PLAY THE PIANO
AND KEYBOARD
MADE EASY

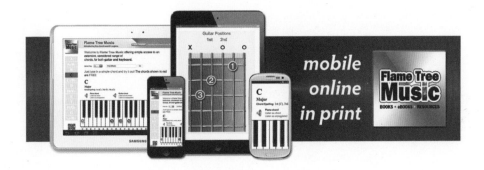

mobile
online
in print

Flame Tree Music
BOOKS • eBOOKS • RESOURCES

© 2013 Flame Tree Publishing Ltd

Publisher and Creative Director: Nick Wells
Project, design and media integration: Jake Jackson
Website and software: David Neville with Stevens Dumpala and Steve Moulton
Editorial: Laura Bulbeck, Emma Chafer and Esme Chapman

Special thanks to: Jane Ashley, Frances Bodiam, Helen Crust,
Christine Delaborde, Stephen Feather, Sara Robson, Chris Herbert, Polly Prior,
Gail Sharkey, Mike Spender and Birgitta Williams.

Alan Brown is a former member of the Scottish National Orchestra. He now works as a freelance musician, with several leading UK
orchestras, and as a consultant in music and IT. Alan has had several compositions published, developed a set of music theory CD-Roms,
co-written a series of bass guitar examination handbooks and worked on over 100 further titles.

Jake Jackson is a writer and musician. He has created and contributed to over 20 practical music books,
including *Reading Music Made Easy*, *Play Flamenco* and *Piano and Keyboard Chords*. His music is available
on iTunes, Amazon and Spotify amongst others.

ISBN: 978-1-4351-5939-6

Manufactured in China

1 3 5 7 9 10 8 6 4 2

PLAY THE PIANO
AND KEYBOARD
MADE EASY

SEE IT █ HEAR IT

COMPREHENSIVE SOUND LINKS

ALAN BROWN WITH JAKE JACKSON

FLAME TREE
PUBLISHING

STEP 1

STEP 2

STEP 3

STEP 4

STEP 5

STEP 6

STEP 7

STEP 8

Contents

FREE ACCESS on smartphones, iPhone, Android etc.
Use any QR code app to scan this QR code

Or go straight to www.flametreemusic.com to
HEAR chords, scales, and find more resources

CONTENTS

STEP 1

STEP 2

STEP 3

STEP 4

STEP 5

STEP 6

STEP 7

STEP 8

FREE ACCESS on smartphones, iPhone, Android etc. Use any QR code app to scan this QR code   Or go straight to www.flametreemusic.com to **HEAR** chords, scales, and find more resources

STEP
1

STEP
2

STEP
3

STEP
4

STEP
5

STEP
6

STEP
7

STEP
8

Play the Piano
An Introduction

This book is divided into 8 sections – the 8 steps to success. If you follow these, and practise regularly, you should be well on the way to mastering this most versatile of instruments.

1.   **Background: Begin Here** gives you a brief introduction to the piano and explains how to take care of it. There are also tips on how to practise. Then will provide advice on how to sit at the piano and how to place your fingers on the keys. It covers the first things you will need to know in order to begin playing the piano.

2.   **The Basics** introduces the staff and clefs (which are used to write music).

3.   **Rhythm & Notes** teaches you about the actual written notes. This is your first step into reading real music.

4.   **Scales & Accidentals** are an important elements of music and this section will show you what these are and how to play and use them.

5.   **Intervals and Chords** are also important. They are particularly important for the left hand as the majority of accompaniments are based in some way on chords.

6.   **Arpeggios** are an extension to chords. They are a very useful tool in order to move around the keyboard fluently. You will meet some music that makes particular use of arpeggios and broken chords.

FREE ACCESS on smartphones, iPhone, Android etc.
Use any QR code app to scan this QR code

Or go straight to www.flametreemusic.com to
HEAR chords, scales, and find more resources

7. **Expression** covers all the elements of a piece of music over and above the pitch and length of the notes. Proper music is so much more than just the notes. This section teaches you the main musical terms in common use so you can understand how a composer wants you to play their music.

8. **Further Techniques** leads you further along the road of performing real music. More key signatures, scales and arpeggios are introduced.

The Next Step is **Going online**. We have designed a dedicated website, flametreemusic.com, which gives chords, scales, resources and play along sheet music to accompany the steps in this book.

• In the **Chords** section of the webiste you can hear the sounds played on the piano both as a chord and an arpeggio.

• In the **Scales** section you can see the notation and hear the scale played.

• The **Resources** section offers recommended reading and links to useful websites.

• The **Pieces** section gives **The Flame Tree Red Book** with sheet music designed to accompany steps in the book, with selections of pieces from famous composers.

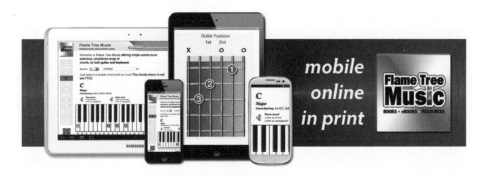

FREE ACCESS on smartphones, iPhone, Android etc. Use any QR code app to scan this QR code

Or go straight to www.flametreemusic.com to **HEAR** chords, scales, and find more resources

STEP 1

STEP 2

STEP 3

STEP 4

STEP 5

STEP 6

STEP 7

STEP 8

STEP 1

STEP 2

STEP 3

STEP 4

STEP 5

STEP 6

STEP 7

STEP 8

Keyboard Diagrams
A Quick Guide

The keyboard diagrams are designed for quick access and ease of use. Whenever you see a keyboard you can use the finger positions and notes to help you make a chord or understand the fingering for a musical example or piece.

Wherever possible the keyboard on the **left** page is for the **left hand**, on the **right** page, the chord is for the **right hand**. This is a great way to learn the structure of the sounds you are making and will help with melodies and solo work.

Tabs help give quick access to each section

Left Hand

Fingering reminder

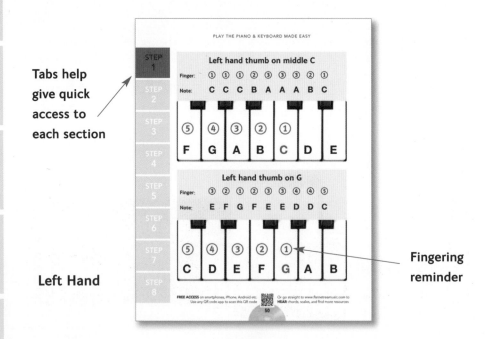

Or go straight to www.flametreemusic.com to **HEAR** chords, scales, and find more resources

Throughout the book the fingers are given numbers:

Left Hand Fingerings:
❶ is the thumb   ❷ is the index finger
❸ is the middle finger   ❹ is the ring finger
❺ is the little finger

Right Hand Fingerings:
❶ is the thumb   ❷ is the index finger
❸ is the middle finger   ❹ is the ring finger
❺ is the little finger

STEP 1
STEP 2
STEP 3
STEP 4
STEP 5
STEP 6
STEP 7
STEP 8

STEP 1: BACKGROUND: BEGIN HERE

Right hand thumb on middle C

Finger:	③	②	①	①	③	②	①	①	①
Note:	E	D	C	C	E	D	C	C	C

STEP 1

① ② ③ ④ ⑤

C D E F G A B

Right Hand

Starting note of the diagram

Right hand thumb on G

Finger:	①	①	②	②	③	③	③	②	①
Note:	G	G	A	A	B	B	B	A	G

① ② ③ ④ ⑤

F G A B C D E

Names of the white notes

FREE ACCESS on smartphones, iPhone, Android etc.
Use any QR code app to scan this QR code

Or go straight to www.flametreemusic.com to
HEAR chords, scales, and find more resources

51

FREE ACCESS on smartphones, iPhone, Android etc.
Use any QR code app to scan this QR code

Or go straight to www.flametreemusic.com to
HEAR chords, scales, and find more resources

The Sound Links
A Quick Guide

Requirements: a camera and internet ready smartphone (eg. **iPhone**, any **Android** phone (e.g. **Samsung** Galaxy), **Nokia Lumia**, or **camera-enabled tablet** such as the **iPad** Mini). The best result is achieved using a WIFI connection.

1. Download any **free QR code reader**. An app store search will reveal a great many of these, so obviously its is best to go with the ones with the highest ratings and don't be afraid to try a few before you settle on the one that works best for you. Tapmedia's QR Reader app is good, or ATT Scanner (used below) or QR Media. Some of the free apps have ads, which can be annoying.

2. Find the chord you want to play, look at the diagram then check out the **QR code** at the base of the page.

FREE ACCESS on smartphones including iPhone & Android   Using any QR code app scan and **HEAR** the chord

76

3. On your smartphone, open the app and **scan** the **QR code** at the base of any particular chord page.

4. The QR reader app will take you to a browser, then the specific chord will be displayed on the flametreemusic.com website.

FREE ACCESS on smartphones, iPhone, Android etc. Use any QR code app to scan this QR code   Or go straight to www.flametreemusic.com to **HEAR** chords, scales, and find more resources

STEP 1
STEP 2
STEP 3
STEP 4
STEP 5
STEP 6
STEP 7
STEP 8

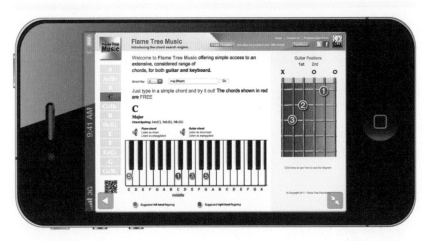

5. Using the usual pinch and zoom techniques, you can focus on four sound options.

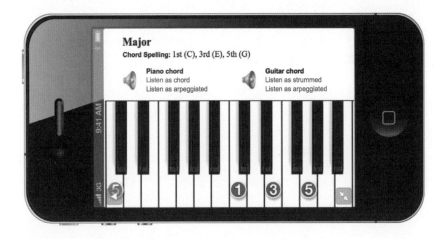

6. Click the sounds! Both piano and guitar audio is provided. This is particularly helpful when you're playing with others.

The QR codes give you direct access to all the chords. You can access a much wider range of chords if you register and subscribe.

FREE ACCESS on smartphones, iPhone, Android etc. Use any QR code app to scan this QR code

Or go straight to www.flametreemusic.com to **HEAR** chords, scales, and find more resources

STEP 1
STEP 2
STEP 3
STEP 4
STEP 5
STEP 6
STEP 7
STEP 8

STEP
1

STEP
2

STEP
3

STEP
4

STEP
5

STEP
6

STEP
7

STEP
8

The Website
flametreemusic.com

The Flame Tree Music web site is designed to make searching for chords very easy. It complements our range of print publications and offers easy access to chords online and on the move, through tablets, smartphones, desktop computers and books.

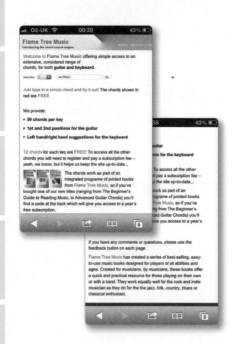

1. The site offers access to chord diagrams and finger positions for both the guitar and the piano/keyboard, presenting a wide range of sound options to help develop good listening technique, and to assist you in identifying the chord and each note within it.

2. The site offers 12 **free** chords, those most commonly used in a band setting or in songwriting.

3. A subscription is available for those who would like access to the full range of chords, 50 for **each key**.

FREE ACCESS on smartphones, iPhone, Android etc. Use any QR code app to scan this QR code

Or go straight to www.flametreemusic.com to **HEAR** chords, scales, and find more resources

4. Guitar chords are shown with **first** and **second positions**.

5. For the keyboard, **left-** and **right-hand positions** are shown. The keyboard also sounds each note.

6. Choose the key, then the chord name from the drop down menu. Note that the **red chords** are available **free**. Those in blue can be accessed with a subscription.

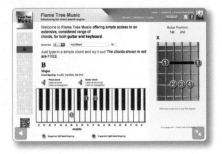

7. Once you've selected the chord, press **GO** and the details of the chord will be shown, with chord spellings, keyboard and guitar fingerings.

8. Initially, the first position for the guitar is shown. The second position can be selected by clicking the text above the chord diagram.

9. Sounds are provided in four easy-to-understand configurations.

We are constantly developing the web site, so further features will be added, including resources, scales and modes.

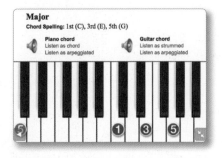

STEP 1
STEP 2
STEP 3
STEP 4
STEP 5
STEP 6
STEP 7
STEP 8

STEP 1

BACKGROUND: BEGIN HERE

It is useful to know how the piano works when you are learning to play it as this will help you understand what is going on when you press a key. This section will give you a basic understanding of the piano and tell you how important it is to look after your instrument and yourself, while playing.

The next few pages will show you the basics of how to play the piano

FREE ACCESS on smartphones, iPhone, Android etc. Use any QR code app to scan this QR code

Or go straight to www.flametreemusic.com to **HEAR** chords, scales, and find more resources

15

STEP 1

STEP 2

STEP 3

STEP 4

STEP 5

STEP 6

STEP 7

STEP 8

STEP
1

STEP
2

STEP
3

STEP
4

STEP
5

STEP
6

STEP
7

STEP
8

The Piano

There have been many different types of keyboard instruments over the years, and the piano is the most recent. Early instruments included the harpsichord, clavichord and spinet (left). In the days before television and computers, the piano was often the centerpiece of the home and families would gather round to listen to music or sing songs. Pianos also offered the main form of respectable public entertainment.

Upright Piano & Electric Piano

Both upright- and grand-style pianos are available, but the upright version is the most common. In an upright piano, the frame and soundboard is vertical, and the strings run vertically across the frame.

The electric piano is played in the same way as an acoustic piano, the only difference being in how the actual sound is made. Electric pianos are smaller as they do not need to have long strings and large soundboards in order to make the sound.

Grand Piano

The grand piano is what you will see in a concert hall. They can range from a baby grand (around 1.2–1.5 m/4–5 ft long) to a full concert grand (up to 2.75 m/9 ft long). The length allows longer strings and a larger soundboard, therefore producing a much larger sound.

Most homes do not have space for a grand piano, so you will probably own either an upright or electric piano.

STEP
1

STEP
2

STEP
3

STEP
4

STEP
5

STEP
6

STEP
7

STEP
8

FREE ACCESS on smartphones, iPhone, Android etc. Use any QR code app to scan this QR code

Or go straight to www.flametreemusic.com to **HEAR** chords, scales, and find more resources

STEP
1

STEP
2

STEP
3

STEP
4

STEP
5

STEP
6

STEP
7

STEP
8

Anatomy of the Piano

A piano consists of many working parts. You will be familiar with the keyboard, but here is a list of the most important parts:

Strings	Hammers
Dampers	Soundboard
Frame	Pedals

When you press the key down, this acts as a lever which in turn pushes a hammer and causes it to hit a string. This is what makes the actual sound.

A '**damper**' rests on the string to stop it from sounding when it is not needed. Pressing a key also releases this damper, which falls back on to the string when you release the key.

If there were only the strings present, the sound would not be very loud. This is where the soundboard comes in – it vibrates in sympathy with the strings and hence amplifies the notes.

How it Works

If you look closely at the photograph below you will be able to see all the internal workings of the piano.

Notice how far from the actual string the key you press is: there are a lot of pivots and levers to enable everything to work together.

You might also see that some notes have just one string, whereas others have two or even three. This is because the higher notes (thinner strings) are not as naturally loud as the lower notes, therefore in order to keep the volume equal across the full range of the piano the higher notes have more strings.

STEP 1

STEP 2

STEP 3

STEP 4

STEP 5

STEP 6

STEP 7

STEP 8

Or go straight to www.flametreemusic.com to **HEAR** chords, scales, and find more resources

STEP 1

STEP 2

STEP 3

STEP 4

STEP 5

STEP 6

STEP 7

STEP 8

Caring for the Piano

Pianos are generally quite robust and are designed to stand being played frequently and for long periods of time. Whether it is an acoustic or an electric model, you should treat it in a similar way to any piece of furniture in your home. Modern pianos cope well with central heating and double glazing, but older models do not fare so well.

In order for a piano to stay in tune, the room needs to be kept at a reasonably constant temperature and humidity. Avoid putting the piano where these things change significantly, such as by a window or a radiator. Try also to keep the piano away from strong sunlight.

You should clean your piano regularly, and you should keep it tuned and in good working condition.

A well-cared-for piano not only sounds better, it will also retain its value and may even increase in value.

Cleaning

Cleaning methods will vary slightly according to what your piano is made from and whether it is an acoustic or electric model, but the general principles apply to both.

For the case, use any standard wood polish or a non-abrasive furniture polish on the outside. If the internal woodwork needs cleaning then use a slightly damp cloth. If you are very careful, and the inside is quite dusty, use a vacuum cleaner on low power and with a soft brush attached.

STEP
1

STEP
2

STEP
3

STEP
4

STEP
5

STEP
6

STEP
7

STEP
8

The actual keyboard should just be wiped with a damp cloth. Avoid using anything abrasive and do not use bleaches. Modern pianos have plastic keys, but older ones may have ivory – you should treat these as you would any antique furniture.

Keep the lid of the piano closed when not in use so that dust cannot easily get in to the piano.

FREE ACCESS on smartphones, iPhone, Android etc. Use any QR code app to scan this QR code

Or go straight to www.flametreemusic.com to **HEAR** chords, scales, and find more resources

21

STEP
1

STEP
2

STEP
3

STEP
4

STEP
5

STEP
6

STEP
7

STEP
8

Tuning

Tuning an acoustic piano is best left to a professional. Not only do you need specialist tools, but you also need a very good ear in order to get the strings in tune with each other.

How often you have a piano tuned depends on several factors, including: how old the piano is; where it is positioned; how often it is played; and how hard it is played. Concert pianos are tuned before every performance, but in the home once every six months to a year is sufficient.

As well as tuning a piano, a good piano tuner will maintain all parts to keep them in good working order. The felt on the hammers can wear down or become flattened after a lot of use, so the sound can be greatly improved by paying attention to this.

It is a good idea to get a full overhaul of a piano if you buy it privately secondhand, but a good piano retailer will ensure this is done for you.

Practising

STEP
1

STEP
2

STEP
3

STEP
4

STEP
5

STEP
6

STEP
7

STEP
8

With any skill, frequency is the key to improvement. Some people will need to spend more time than others, and there are always some for whom it all comes naturally.

How Often Should I Practise?

Ideally you should develop a **daily routine**. Not necessarily all the same things every day, but maybe have a few regular exercises or scales to keep the fingers supple and build up stamina and technique. Then rotate through the pieces you are learning.

FREE ACCESS on smartphones, iPhone, Android etc. Use any QR code app to scan this QR code

Or go straight to www.flametreemusic.com to **HEAR** chords, scales, and find more resources

23

STEP
1

STEP
2

STEP
3

STEP
4

STEP
5

STEP
6

STEP
7

STEP
8

How Long Should I Practise For?

As suggested already, frequency is the key to success rather than pure length of practice time. You will progress much faster with **seven daily 20-minute sessions** during the week rather than just one long session of 2 hours and 20 minutes.

You need to balance the length of practice with the time available and the amount of material you are trying to learn. Do not be over-optimistic as you are likely to put it off if you plan sessions that are too long.

For a complete beginner, **10 to 15 minutes every day** is enough. This way it does not become a chore but you are eased in to the idea of practice gently. It should be fun. Build up to half an hour every day.

Don't forget, this is serious **practice** time. Playing through your pieces or improvising should also be done as often as you can make time. This can be just as relaxing as watching TV, and often much more fulfilling.

Using a Metronome

Playing in time and rhythmically is important, particularly if you are ever going to play along with anyone else. You will be concentrating hard on playing all the right notes so the timing is often neglected. A metronome can help, by providing a consistent rhythmic pulse to play along to. There are several ways a metronome can help:

- Avoiding playing easy passages quicker than harder passages.

- Playing a piece at the speed a composer intended.

- Helping with learning difficult passages by playing through at a steady pace, then increasing the speed very slightly for each successive play-through.

Whether to use a traditional mechanical metronome or a modern electronic one is a matter of choice – an old wooden one looks nice, whereas an electric one will fit in your pocket.

STEP 1

STEP 2

STEP 3

STEP 4

STEP 5

STEP 6

STEP 7

STEP 8

Please Sit!

STEP 1

STEP 2

STEP 3

STEP 4

STEP 5

STEP 6

STEP 7

STEP 8

It is important to be comfortable when sitting at the piano. You should also be easily able to reach all the notes you will need to play.

A piano stool is the most common thing people sit on, but a chair is quite adequate providing it does not slope and it has no arm rests.

Your feet should rest on the floor (though this is not always possible if you are small!) and your back should be straight. **Do not lean back**.

Your forearms should be horizontal and your **shoulders loose**, allowing your fingers to touch the keys comfortably without stretching. Imagine your hands floating along the keyboard, just touching the keys.

FREE ACCESS on smartphones, iPhone, Android etc. Use any QR code app to scan this QR code

Or go straight to www.flametreemusic.com to **HEAR** chords, scales, and find more resources

STEP
1

STEP
2

STEP
3

STEP
4

STEP
5

STEP
6

STEP
7

STEP
8

FREE ACCESS on smartphones, iPhone, Android etc. Use any QR code app to scan this QR code

Or go straight to www.flametreemusic.com to **HEAR** chords, scales, and find more resources

STEP
1

STEP
2

STEP
3

STEP
4

STEP
5

STEP
6

STEP
7

STEP
8

Feet and Pedals

Position your piano stool so that you do not have to lean forward in order to play the keys. Your feet should also easily reach the pedals without stretching. But do not sit so close that you feel scrunched up. You need space for your arms and hands to move freely along the keyboard.

When not using the pedals, your feet should rest on the floor just in front of the pedals. You should just need to move your foot forwards a little in order to press a pedal.

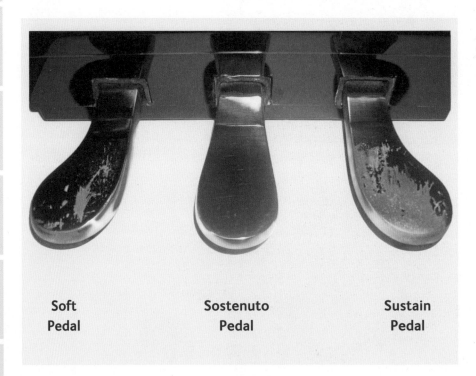

| Soft
Pedal | Sostenuto
Pedal | Sustain
Pedal |

FREE ACCESS on smartphones, iPhone, Android etc. Use any QR code app to scan this QR code Or go straight to www.flametreemusic.com to **HEAR** chords, scales, and find more resources

28

If your legs are not long enough to reach the pedals do not worry too much as they are not essential at this stage. If you want to experiment with them, then just slide forward on your stool until you can reach them. Just press the pedals lightly – do not stand on them.

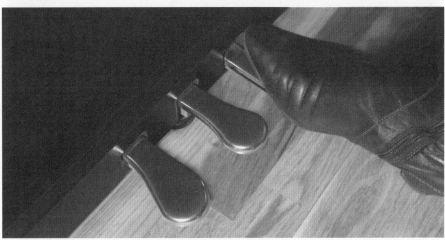

STEP 1

STEP 2

STEP 3

STEP 4

STEP 5

STEP 6

STEP 7

STEP 8

STEP 1

STEP 2

STEP 3

STEP 4

STEP 5

STEP 6

STEP 7

STEP 8

FREE ACCESS on smartphones, iPhone, Android etc.
Use any QR code app to scan this QR code

Or go straight to www.flametreemusic.com to
HEAR chords, scales, and find more resources

Hands Please

Remember, your audience wants to hear the music – not a clicking of nails on the keys.

You will need to keep your nails reasonably short, but do not over-do it. **Play** the keys with the part of your **finger between** the **tip** and the **pad**.

Your fingers should curve gently on to the keys. Avoid straight fingers, but do not curl them up too much. Imagine your hand is a spider which needs to run along the keyboard. You can go much faster if your **fingers** are **curved** and **relaxed**.

To get the position you are aiming for, try this:

- Let a tennis ball rest in the palm of your hand, with your fingers touching it all round.

- Relax a little and remove the ball.

- Now turn your hand over; this is the position you need.

FREE ACCESS on smartphones, iPhone, Android etc. Use any QR code app to scan this QR code

Or go straight to www.flametreemusic.com to **HEAR** chords, scales, and find more resources

31

STEP 1
STEP 2
STEP 3
STEP 4
STEP 5
STEP 6
STEP 7
STEP 8

STEP 1

STEP 2

STEP 3

STEP 4

STEP 5

STEP 6

STEP 7

STEP 8

Warming Up

Try some warm-up exercises to loosen your fingers before you start your main practice session. A few slow scales and some simple stretching exercises are good.

If your hands are cold then do not stretch too far too soon. Play a few notes, then **shake** your **hands** to release any tension.

If you can see or feel your hands becoming tense, stop and shake them loose. **Playing should be** as **relaxed** as possible and it certainly should not look like hard work.

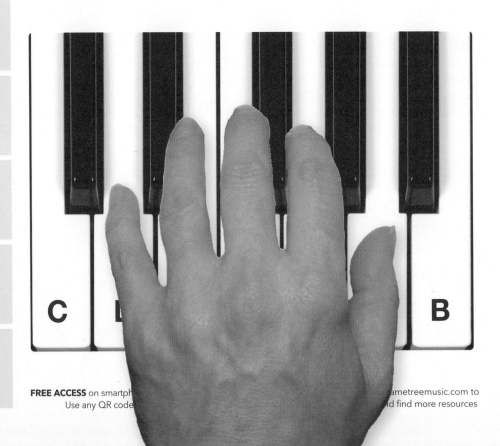

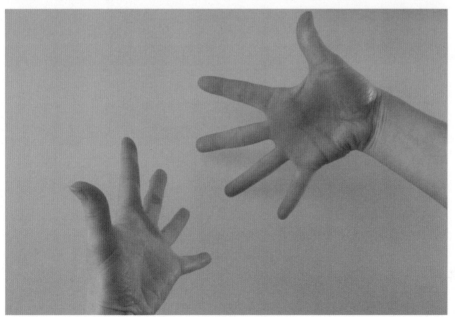

FREE ACCESS on smartphones, iPhone, Android etc.
Use any QR code app to scan this QR code

Or go straight to www.flametreemusic.com to
HEAR chords, scales, and find more resources

33

STEP 1

STEP 2

STEP 3

STEP 4

STEP 5

STEP 6

STEP 7

STEP 8

STEP
1

STEP
2

STEP
3

STEP
4

STEP
5

STEP
6

STEP
7

STEP
8

Notes on the Keyboard

We are now going to have a look at the notes on the keyboard of the instrument.

White Notes

The white notes on the piano are given letter names, but we only use the first seven letters of the standard alphabet.

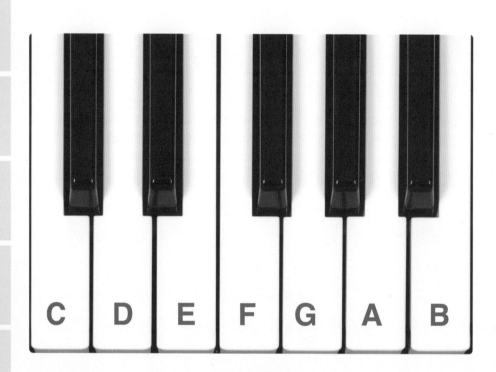

FREE ACCESS on smartphones, iPhone, Android etc.
Use any QR code app to scan this QR code

Or go straight to www.flametreemusic.com to
HEAR chords, scales, and find more resources

34

A   B   C   D   E   F   and   G

When you get to G you start again from A.

STEP
1

STEP
2

STEP
3

STEP
4

STEP
5

STEP
6

STEP
7

STEP
8

The simplest **major scale** is just **all** the **white notes** played one after the other, but starting from **C**. Try playing these notes and listen to the sound made.

If you play any three alternate notes together then these will make up what we call a **chord**. Try a few and hear what chords sound like. **This one is C major.**

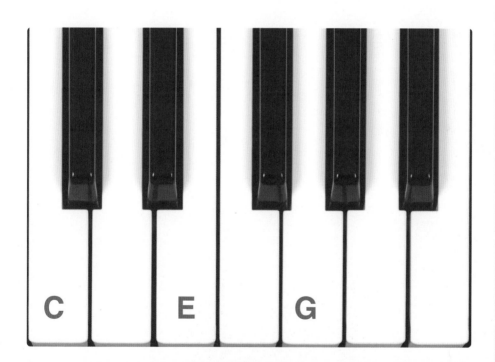

FREE ACCESS on smartphones, iPhone, Android etc.
Use any QR code app to scan this QR code

Or go straight to www.flametreemusic.com to
HEAR chords, scales, and find more resources

35

Black Notes

STEP 1

STEP 2

STEP 3

STEP 4

STEP 5

STEP 6

STEP 7

STEP 8

In between most of the white notes you will find black notes. These are the sharps and flats.

Sharp sign   Flat sign

Or go straight to www.flametreemusic.com to **HEAR** chords, scales, and find more resources

STEP
1

STEP
2

STEP
3

STEP
4

STEP
5

STEP
6

STEP
7

STEP
8

All the black notes can be referred to by two different names, depending on the key you are in. This really depends on which main (white) note you want to compare the black note to.

If you want to refer to a note as 'being a little **higher** than F' then you will call it **F sharp**. When you compare it to G (a little **lower** than G) you would call it a **G flat**.

You get '**higher**' by going to the **right** on the keyboard and '**lower**' by going to the **left**.

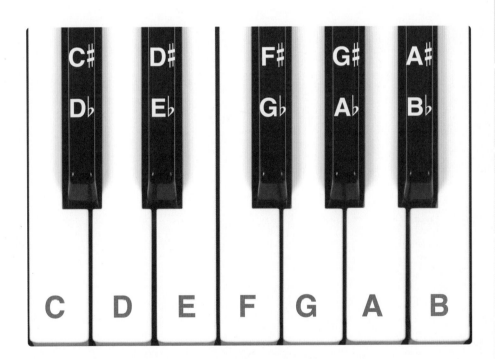

FREE ACCESS on smartphones, iPhone, Android etc. Use any QR code app to scan this QR code

Or go straight to www.flametreemusic.com to **HEAR** chords, scales, and find more resources

**STEP
1**

**STEP
2**

**STEP
3**

**STEP
4**

**STEP
5**

**STEP
6**

**STEP
7**

**STEP
8**

Finger Numbers

We need some way of knowing which finger to use on which note. It would become very difficult to read the music if we used names such as thumb, index finger, and so on. Instead, we give each finger a number. That way, if a note should be played with the middle finger you would see a number 3 above the note on the music.

Both hands have their **thumb** and **fingers** numbered from **1 to 5**, starting with the thumb.

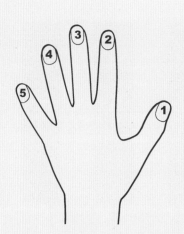
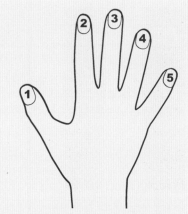

**Don't forget, the thumb on both hands is finger number 1
and the little finger is finger number 5.**

FREE ACCESS on smartphones, iPhone, Android etc.
Use any QR code app to scan this QR code

Or go straight to www.flametreemusic.com to
HEAR chords, scales, and find more resources

38

STEP 1

STEP 2

STEP 3

STEP 4

STEP 5

STEP 6

STEP 7

STEP 8

FREE ACCESS on smartphones, iPhone, Android etc. Use any QR code app to scan this QR code

Or go straight to www.flametreemusic.com to **HEAR** chords, scales, and find more resources

STEP 1

STEP 2

STEP 3

STEP 4

STEP 5

STEP 6

STEP 7

STEP 8

Finger Numbers for the Left Hand

Left Hand

Finger Numbers for the Right Hand

Right Hand

STEP
1

STEP
2

STEP
3

STEP
4

STEP
5

STEP
6

STEP
7

STEP
8

STEP
1

STEP
2

STEP
3

STEP
4

STEP
5

STEP
6

STEP
7

STEP
8

Five-finger Position

Left Hand on the Keyboard

This illustration shows which finger to put on which notes for the **left hand** exercises you will be given shortly.

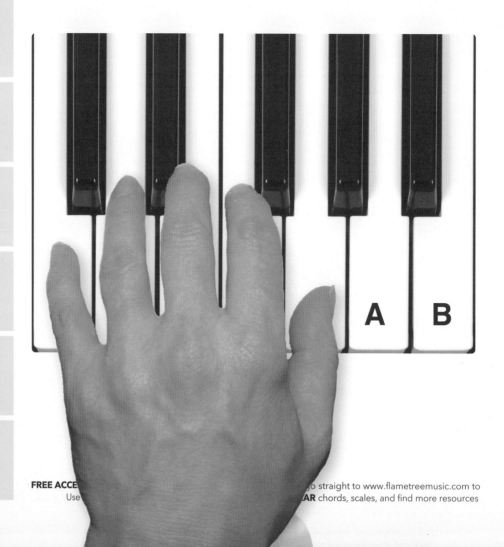

Right Hand on the Keyboard

This illustration shows which finger to put on which notes for the **right hand** exercises you will be given shortly.

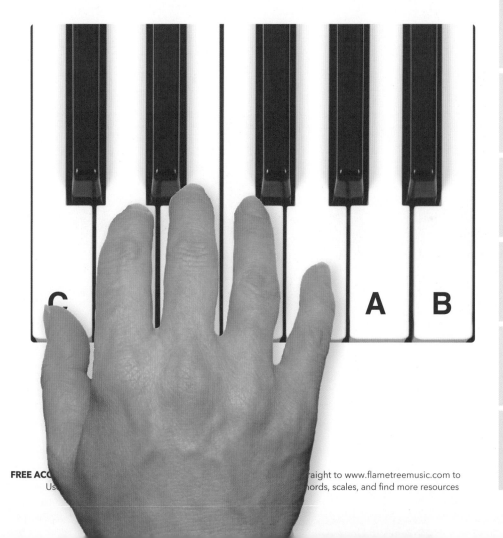

STEP 1

STEP 2

STEP 3

STEP 4

STEP 5

STEP 6

STEP 7

STEP 8

Very First Tunes

Simple Tunes for the Left Hand

Place your fingers on the keys, then press the finger numbers shown one at a time. The keyboard diagram will help you see which notes should be used.

STEP 1

STEP 2

STEP 3

STEP 4

STEP 5

STEP 6

STEP 7

STEP 8

FREE ACCESS on smartphones, iPhone, Android etc. Use any QR code app to scan this QR code Or go straight to www.flametreemusic.com to **HEAR** chords, scales, and find more resources

STEP
1

STEP
2

STEP
3

STEP
4

STEP
5

STEP
6

STEP
7

STEP
8

Simple Tunes for the Right Hand

Now for the right hand. Place your fingers on the keys, then press the finger numbers shown one at a time.

①	②	①	②		①	②	③	④		⑤
③	②	①	①		③	④	⑤	⑤		⑤
⑤	④	④	③		②	③	②	②		①

①　②　③　④　⑤

FREE ACCESS on smartphones, iPhone, Android etc. Use any QR code app to scan this QR code

Or go straight to www.flametreemusic.com to **HEAR** chords, scales, and find more resources

45

What We Know So Far

STEP
2

STEP
3

STEP
4

STEP
5

STEP
6

STEP
7

STEP
8

1. You should **always sit comfortably** – not needing to stretch to reach the keys or the pedals.

2. **Fingers** should be **gently curved**.

3. There are white keys with the letter names **A**, **B**, **C**, **D**, **E**, **F** and **G**.

4. Black keys are sometimes called **sharps** and sometimes called **flats**.

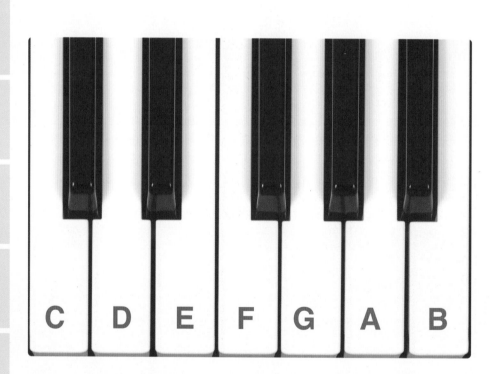

FREE ACCESS on smartphones, iPhone, Android etc.
Use any QR code app to scan this QR code

Or go straight to www.flametreemusic.com to
HEAR chords, scales, and find more resources

STEP
1

STEP
2

STEP
3

STEP
4

STEP
5

STEP
6

STEP
7

STEP
8

5. **Fingers** are **numbered** from 1 to 5, starting with the **thumb** on each hand.

6. **Always warm up** before playing.

7. Practice is more effective when you do **lots of small sessions** rather than one big one.

8. Try to **play every day**.

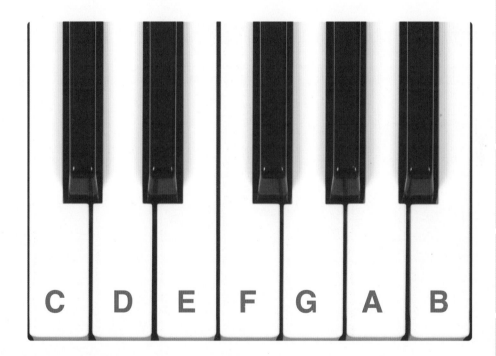

FREE ACCESS on smartphones, iPhone, Android etc. Use any QR code app to scan this QR code Or go straight to www.flametreemusic.com to **HEAR** chords, scales, and find more resources

47

STEP 1

STEP 2

STEP 3

STEP 4

STEP 5

STEP 6

STEP 7

STEP 8

Now Try This

Try the simple tunes on the next few pages. We will start off with a few single-hand tunes before we try putting the hands together.

Playing by Numbers

Place your thumb on the note indicated in red, then have one finger per note for the other fingers. When a tune starts on 'middle C', this is the C nearest the middle of your keyboard; if your piano has a lock, then middle C is just near this.

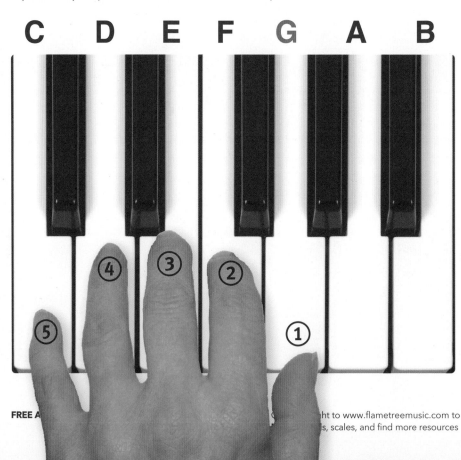

C   D   E   F   G   A   B

STEP 1

STEP 2

STEP 3

STEP 4

STEP 5

STEP 6

STEP 7

STEP 8

The first few tunes should be played with even notes – all having the same length. When we come to putting the hands together you will see that the left hand has one note to play while the right hand has four. Hold the left hand finger down while the right hand plays its notes.

The last tunes in this section mix things up, using both hands, with long and short notes. Use these as inspiration for improvizing extra bars that complement them, so that it all sounds like one piece. It does not matter where you start on the keyboard for improvization, the important thing is that you listen to the sound. Try starting on all different notes, maybe even try all black notes.

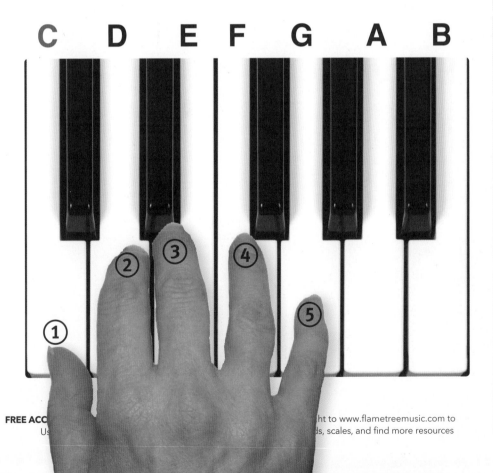

STEP 1
STEP 2
STEP 3
STEP 4
STEP 5
STEP 6
STEP 7
STEP 8

Left hand thumb on middle C

Finger:	①	①	①	②	③	③	③	②	①
Note:	C	C	C	B	A	A	A	B	C

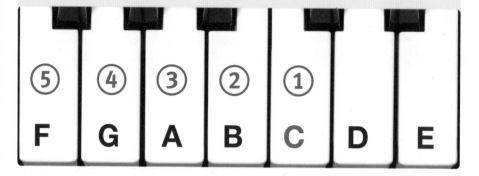

⑤ F ④ G ③ A ② B ① C D E

Left hand thumb on G

Finger:	③	②	①	②	③	③	④	④	⑤
Note:	E	F	G	F	E	E	D	D	C

⑤ C ④ D ③ E ② F ① G A B

FREE ACCESS on smartphones, iPhone, Android etc.
Use any QR code app to scan this QR code

Or go straight to www.flametreemusic.com to
HEAR chords, scales, and find more resources

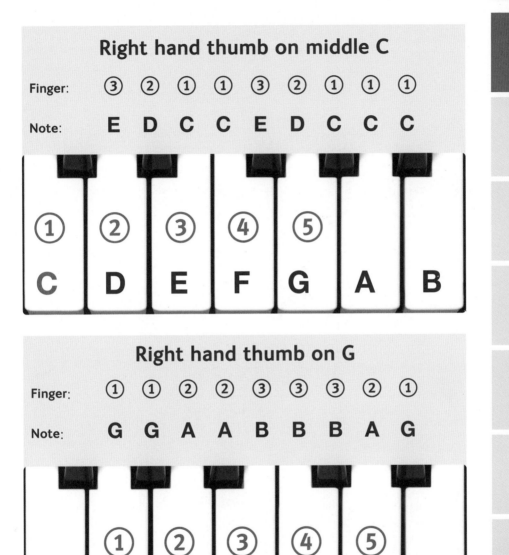

STEP 1
STEP 2
STEP 3
STEP 4
STEP 5
STEP 6
STEP 7
STEP 8

Or go straight to www.flametreemusic.com to **HEAR** chords, scales, and find more resources

STEP 1

STEP 2

STEP 3

STEP 4

STEP 5

STEP 6

STEP 7

STEP 8

Now with hands together, but using the same finger in each hand at the same time.

Both thumbs on middle C

R finger:	①	①	①	②	③	③	③	②	①
R note:	C	C	C	D	E	E	E	D	C
L finger:	①	①	①	②	③	③	③	②	①
L note:	C	C	C	B	A	A	A	B	C

Right hand thumb on a high G, left hand thumb on a low G

R finger:	①	③	⑤	③	④	③	②	②	①
R note:	G	B	D	B	C	B	A	A	G
L finger:	①	③	⑤	③	④	③	②	②	①
L note:	G	E	C	E	D	E	F	F	G

Hands together, again playing the same note in each hand at the same time.

Right hand thumb on middle C, left hand thumb on G

R finger:	①	①	②	②	③	③	④	⑤	①
R note:	C	C	D	D	E	E	F	G	C
L finger:	⑤	⑤	④	④	③	③	②	①	⑤
L note:	C	C	D	D	E	E	F	G	C

Right hand thumb on G, left hand thumb on D

R finger:	①	⑤	①	⑤	①	③	⑤	③	①
R note:	G	D	G	D	G	B	D	B	G
L finger:	⑤	①	⑤	①	⑤	③	①	③	⑤
L note:	G	D	G	D	G	B	D	B	G

STEP 1
STEP 2
STEP 3
STEP 4
STEP 5
STEP 6
STEP 7
STEP 8

STEP
1

STEP
2

STEP
3

STEP
4

STEP
5

STEP
6

STEP
7

STEP
8

Hands together, but now the left hand is playing long notes.

Right hand thumb on middle C, left hand thumb on G

R finger:	③	②	③	②	⑤	④	⑤	④	①
R note:	E	D	E	D	G	F	G	F	C
L finger:	⑤				①				⑤
L note:	C				G				C

Right hand thumb on middle D, left hand thumb on A

R finger:	①	①	②	③	⑤	⑤	④	②	①
R note:	D	D	E	F	A	A	G	E	D
L finger:	⑤				①		①		⑤
L note:	D				A		A		D

FREE ACCESS on smartphones, iPhone, Android etc.
Use any QR code app to scan this QR code

Or go straight to www.flametreemusic.com to
HEAR chords, scales, and find more resources

54

Now let's mix all these things up.

Right hand thumb on middle C, left hand thumb on G

R finger:	③	④	③	②	③	⑤	③	②	①
R note:	E	F	E	D	E	G	E	D	C
L finger:	③	④	③	②	①		①		⑤
L note:	E	D	E	F	G		G		C

Right hand thumb on a very high A, left hand thumb on a very low E

R finger:	①	①	⑤	⑤	③	③	⑤	⑤	①
R note:	A	A	E	E	C	C	E	E	A
L finger:	⑤	⑤	①	①	③	③	①		⑤
L note:	A	A	E	E	C	C	E		A

STEP 1
STEP 2
STEP 3
STEP 4
STEP 5
STEP 6
STEP 7
STEP 8

STEP 2

THE BASICS

We need some way for a composer to tell the player what notes to play and how to play them. This is the written music. Music is written using specific shapes and lines placed on a set of five lines called a stave or staff. Higher notes are placed higher up the staff and lower notes are placed lower down.

You will come across lots of different symbols and musical terms as you learn the piano, but there are not too many essential ones to get you started.

STEP
1

STEP
2

STEP
3

STEP
4

STEP
5

STEP
6

STEP
7

STEP
8

FREE ACCESS on smartphones, iPhone, Android etc. Use any QR code app to scan this QR code

Or go straight to www.flametreemusic.com to **HEAR** chords, scales, and find more resources

The Staff

STEP 1

STEP 2

STEP 3

STEP 4

STEP 5

STEP 6

STEP 7

STEP 8

Music is written on a series of five lines, called the stave or staff. The notes are either placed on a line or in a space to indicate which pitch to play.

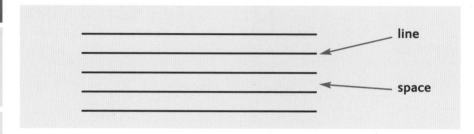

For piano, we use two sets of these lines: **one** for the **right** hand and **one** for the **left** hand. They are placed one above the other and are bracketed together to show that the hands play together.

STEP 1

STEP 2

STEP 3

STEP 4

STEP 5

STEP 6

STEP 7

STEP 8

Music is read the same way as words on a page – from left to right, then down the page starting at the top.

The music is grouped into **bars**, and you will see vertical lines regularly throughout the music. This makes the music easier to follow and also indicates the basic rhythmic pulse, but we will go in to that later.

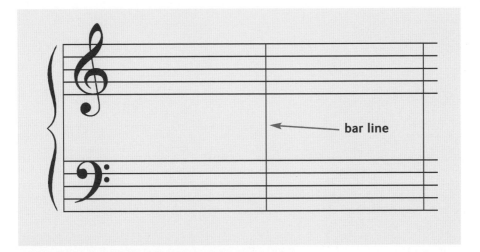

bar line

FREE ACCESS on smartphones, iPhone, Android etc. Use any QR code app to scan this QR code

Or go straight to www.flametreemusic.com to **HEAR** chords, scales, and find more resources

59

The Treble Clef

STEP
1

STEP
2

STEP
3

STEP
4

STEP
5

STEP
6

STEP
7

STEP
8

There are special symbols to indicate the type of staff being used: five static lines are not enough to cover the whole piano. We will only need to learn two symbols for the piano.

The first symbol is the **treble clef**. It is generally used for the right hand. It is used for **music above middle C**.

FREE ACCESS on smartphones, iPhone, Android etc.
Use any QR code app to scan this QR code

Or go straight to www.flametreemusic.com to
HEAR chords, scales, and find more resources

60

Middle C is the C on the keyboard closest to the **middle** of the **keyboard**.

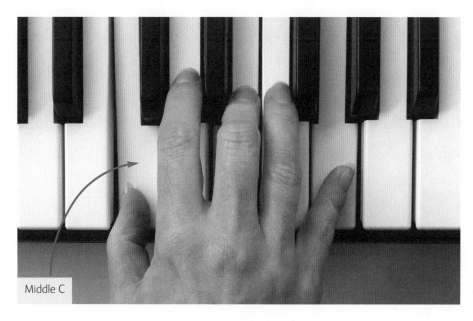

Middle C

The treble clef is sometimes called the '**G clef**' because you start to draw it from the **G line** on the stave. You will learn the names of the lines and spaces shortly.

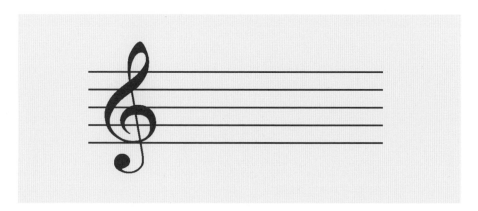

STEP 1

STEP 2

STEP 3

STEP 4

STEP 5

STEP 6

STEP 7

STEP 8

STEP 1

STEP 2

STEP 3

STEP 4

STEP 5

STEP 6

STEP 7

STEP 8

The Lines of the Treble Clef

The names of the five lines in the treble clef are (starting from the lowest) E, G, B, D and F. See if you can find these notes on your keyboard.

It is difficult to remember the letters to begin with so we often use a simple phrase to remind us, with the first letter of each word being the letter name of the line.

Here are two common phrases. Pick your favourite, or make up your own by filling in the gaps below.

Every Green Bus Drives Fast

Every Good Boy Deserves Football

E _ _ _   G _ _ _   B _ _ _   D _ _ _ F _ _ _

Here is a note on a line:

STEP 1

STEP 2

STEP 3

STEP 4

STEP 5

STEP 6

STEP 7

STEP 8

STEP 1

STEP 2

STEP 3

STEP 4

STEP 5

STEP 6

STEP 7

STEP 8

The Spaces of the Treble Clef

As with the lines, we need a way of remembering the spaces between the lines.

There are just **four spaces** and in the **treble clef** they just happen to make up a word:

F A C E

This is an easy one to remember.

FREE ACCESS on smartphones, iPhone, Android etc.
Use any QR code app to scan this QR code

Or go straight to www.flametreemusic.com to
HEAR chords, scales, and find more resources

64

Try playing all these four notes together on the piano – they make quite a nice sound. A **chord**.

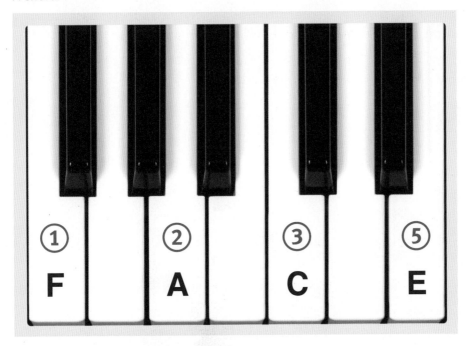

Here is what a note in a **space** looks like:

FREE ACCESS on smartphones, iPhone, Android etc. Use any QR code app to scan this QR code

Or go straight to www.flametreemusic.com to **HEAR** chords, scales, and find more resources

STEP 1

STEP 2

STEP 3

STEP 4

STEP 5

STEP 6

STEP 7

STEP 8

The Bass Clef

STEP 1

STEP 2

STEP 3

STEP 4

STEP 5

STEP 6

STEP 7

STEP 8

For the lower notes we need to use a different clef. The bass clef covers the notes below middle C and is generally used for the left hand.

On the piano we need to know both the treble and bass clefs as we can play both high and low notes, using the left and right hands.

Or go straight to www.flametreemusic.com to **HEAR** chords, scales, and find more resources

STEP
1

**STEP
2**

STEP
3

STEP
4

STEP
5

STEP
6

STEP
7

STEP
8

Many other instruments just use one of the clefs as they can only play high or only play low. Look at these instruments below, then see if you can work out whether they will use the treble or bass clef.

The bass clef is sometimes known as the F clef as you begin to draw it from **the F line** on the stave.

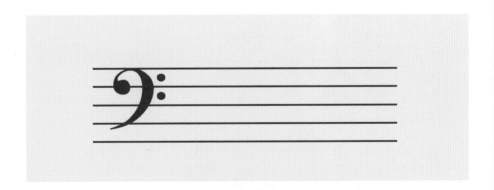

FREE ACCESS on smartphones, iPhone, Android etc.
Use any QR code app to scan this QR code

Or go straight to www.flametreemusic.com to
HEAR chords, scales, and find more resources

67

STEP
1

STEP
2

STEP
3

STEP
4

STEP
5

STEP
6

STEP
7

STEP
8

The Lines of the Bass Clef

As with the treble clef, we need a way to remember the names of the **five lines** of the bass clef.

They are **different** to the treble clef – the bass clef lines (starting at the bottom) are:

G B D F A

This one is not so easy to remember, but just as important.

FREE ACCESS on smartphones, iPhone, Android etc. Use any QR code app to scan this QR code   Or go straight to www.flametreemusic.com to **HEAR** chords, scales, and find more resources

Here are some phrases to help you remember them:

Good Boys Don't Forget Anything

Good Boys Do Fine Always

Why not try to make up your own?

G _ _ _ B _ _ _ D _ _ _ F _ _ _ A _ _ _

Here is a note on a **line**:

STEP 1

STEP 2

STEP 3

STEP 4

STEP 5

STEP 6

STEP 7

STEP 8

STEP 1

STEP 2

STEP 3

STEP 4

STEP 5

STEP 6

STEP 7

STEP 8

The Spaces of the Bass Clef

We also need a way of remembering the spaces.

As in the treble clef, there are just **four spaces** in the **bass clef**, starting at the bottom.

A C E G

This is also an easy one to remember.

FREE ACCESS on smartphones, iPhone, Android etc. Use any QR code app to scan this QR code

Or go straight to www.flametreemusic.com to **HEAR** chords, scales, and find more resources

70

Here are some phrases to help you remember them:

All Cows Eat Grass

All Cars Eat Gas

Now try to make up your own.

A _ _ _   C _ _ _   E _ _ _   G _ _ _

Here is a note in a space:

FREE ACCESS on smartphones, iPhone, Android etc. Use any QR code app to scan this QR code

Or go straight to www.flametreemusic.com to **HEAR** chords, scales, and find more resources

STEP 1

STEP 2

STEP 3

STEP 4

STEP 5

STEP 6

STEP 7

STEP 8

STEP
1

STEP
2

STEP
3

STEP
4

STEP
5

STEP
6

STEP
7

STEP
8

Skips and Steps

Music is made up of notes moving step by step at different speeds or by jumping over notes, often called skipping.

It is important to get to know both these things, and the following pages have some exercises for you to try.

For the **step-by-step** exercises, place the finger indicated on the starting note then try to use just one finger per note **without moving your hand** at all during the exercise.

For the **skipping exercises**, try two methods.

1.   Firstly try to play all the notes by hardly moving the hand – stretch for the notes.

2.   Then try skipping along the notes using just one to two fingers.

How about trying each one five times, once for each finger?

FREE ACCESS on smartphones, iPhone, Android etc.
Use any QR code app to scan this QR code

Or go straight to www.flametreemusic.com to
HEAR chords, scales, and find more resources

STEP
1

STEP
2

STEP
3

STEP
4

STEP
5

STEP
6

STEP
7

STEP
8

FREE ACCESS on smartphones, iPhone, Android etc. Use any QR code app to scan this QR code

Or go straight to www.flametreemusic.com to **HEAR** chords, scales, and find more resources

STEP 1

STEP 2

STEP 3

STEP 4

STEP 5

STEP 6

STEP 7

STEP 8

Right Hand Steps

Place your thumb on G

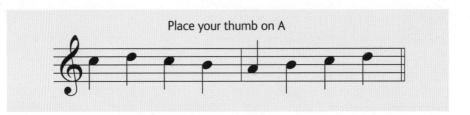

Place your thumb on A

Right Hand Skips

Place your thumb on E

Place your thumb on B

FREE ACCESS on smartphones, iPhone, Android etc. Use any QR code app to scan this QR code

Or go straight to www.flametreemusic.com to **HEAR** chords, scales, and find more resources

Left Hand Steps

Place your thumb on G

Place your thumb on D

Left Hand Skips

Place your thumb on F

Place your thumb on G

STEP 1
STEP 2
STEP 3
STEP 4
STEP 5
STEP 6
STEP 7
STEP 8

STEP
1

STEP
2

STEP
3

STEP
4

STEP
5

STEP
6

STEP
7

STEP
8

Steps and Skips for Right Hand

Start with your thumb on G, but watch out for the big jumps at the end.

FREE ACCESS on smartphones, iPhone, Android etc.
Use any QR code app to scan this QR code

Or go straight to www.flametreemusic.com to
HEAR chords, scales, and find more resources

76

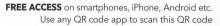

Steps and Skips for Left Hand

Start with your thumb on G, but watch out for the big jumps at the end.

STEP
1

STEP
2

STEP
3

STEP
4

STEP
5

STEP
6

STEP
7

STEP
8

This is middle C

STEP
1

STEP
2

STEP
3

STEP
4

STEP
5

STEP
6

STEP
7

STEP
8

Playing by Ear

There are times when written music is not available. For example, you might hear a piece of music at a concert and want to play it yourself. Or maybe a friend has worked out a great song but doesn't know how to write music. This is where playing by ear is a useful skill.

As the term implies, your ear is as important as your fingers. You need to listen carefully to the music played, then try to copy it on the piano.

Here are some specific things to ask yourself:

1.   **Is the music high or low?**

2.   **Is the music fast or slow?**

3.   **Do the notes move step by step or skip along?**

4.   **How far apart do the notes sound?**

FREE ACCESS on smartphones, iPhone, Android etc.
Use any QR code app to scan this QR code

Or go straight to www.flametreemusic.com to
HEAR chords, scales, and find more resources

STEP
1

STEP
2

STEP
3

STEP
4

STEP
5

STEP
6

STEP
7

STEP
8

Create a **shape** in your mind then try to recreate this on the piano.

The exercises on the following pages give you some practice at playing by ear; the first stage of creating a **shape diagram** has been done for you.

Try starting on a **different note each time** you play these shapes.

You might come across these tunes later in this book, so be on the look-out!

FREE ACCESS on smartphones, iPhone, Android etc. Use any QR code app to scan this QR code Or go straight to www.flametreemusic.com to **HEAR** chords, scales, and find more resources

79

STEP
1

STEP
2

STEP
3

STEP
4

STEP
5

STEP
6

STEP
7

STEP
8

Left Hand Tunes

Gently flowing

Jumping around

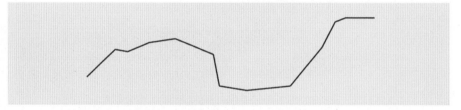

Steps in groups

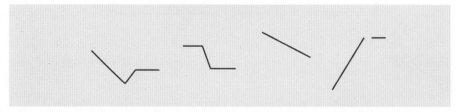

Where you see a horizontal, play the same note several times.

FREE ACCESS on smartphones, iPhone, Android etc.
Use any QR code app to scan this QR code

Or go straight to www.flametreemusic.com to
HEAR chords, scales, and find more resources

Right Hand Tunes

Gently flowing

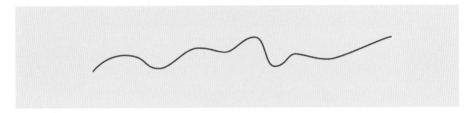

Jumping around

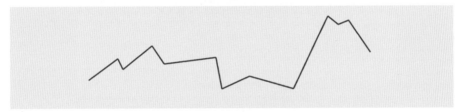

Steps in groups

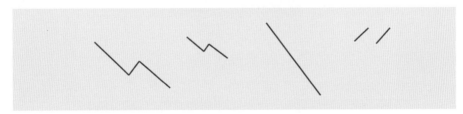

Where there is a gap, jump to a new starting note.

STEP 1

STEP 2

STEP 3

STEP 4

STEP 5

STEP 6

STEP 7

STEP 8

STEP 1

STEP 2

STEP 3

STEP 4

STEP 5

STEP 6

STEP 7

STEP 8

Tunes for Both Hands

Echoes

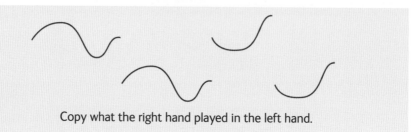

Copy what the right hand played in the left hand.

Jumping together

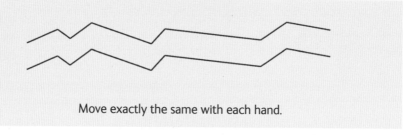

Move exactly the same with each hand.

Black note bounce

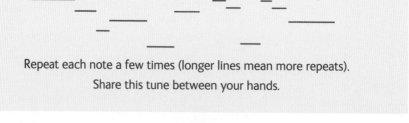

Repeat each note a few times (longer lines mean more repeats).
Share this tune between your hands.

FREE ACCESS on smartphones, iPhone, Android etc.
Use any QR code app to scan this QR code

Or go straight to www.flametreemusic.com to
HEAR chords, scales, and find more resources

Question and Answer

Here are the beginnings of 4 phrases. Make up a **second half** for each so that it either copies or mirrors the start you are given.

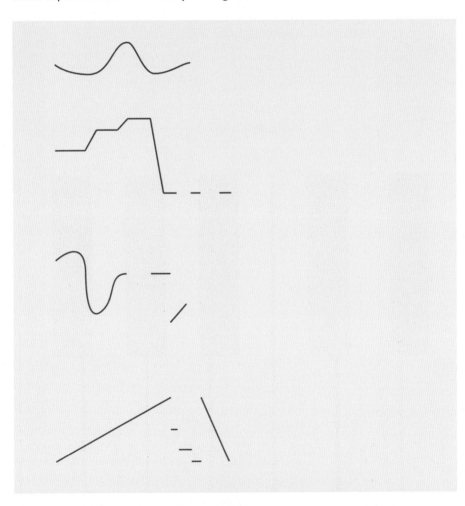

STEP
1

STEP
2

STEP
3

STEP
4

STEP
5

STEP
6

STEP
7

STEP
8

  Or go straight to www.flametreemusic.com to **HEAR** chords, scales, and find more resources

STEP 1

STEP 2

STEP 3

STEP 4

STEP 5

STEP 6

STEP 7

STEP 8

What We Know So Far

We have gone a long way from just playing by numbers. You can now read music and play by ear. Here is a reminder of what you should know:

1. Music is written on five lines called a stave or a **staff**.

2. Notes are either on the **lines** or in the **spaces**.

3. Every line and every space has a **letter name**.

FREE ACCESS on smartphones, iPhone, Android etc. Use any QR code app to scan this QR code

Or go straight to www.flametreemusic.com to **HEAR** chords, scales, and find more resources

84

STEP
1

STEP
2

STEP
3

STEP
4

STEP
5

STEP
6

STEP
7

STEP
8

4. The higher notes are written on a staff with a **treble** clef.

5. The lower notes are written on a staff with a **bass** clef.

6. You have learned **phrases** to remind you of the letter names of the lines and spaces.

7. Playing by ear involves **listening** carefully to the music and creating a melodic 'shape'.

8. Music moves from note to note either **step by step** or by **skipping** from one note to the next.

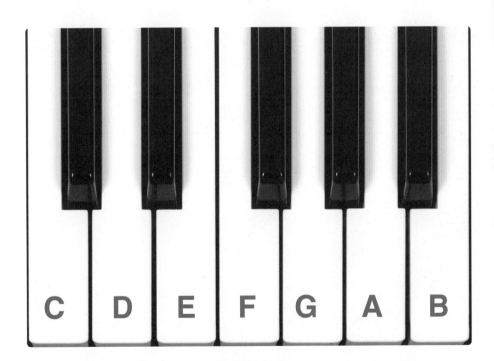

C D E F G A B

FREE ACCESS on smartphones, iPhone, Android etc. Use any QR code app to scan this QR code

Or go straight to www.flametreemusic.com to **HEAR** chords, scales, and find more resources

85

Now Try This

STEP 1

STEP 2

STEP 3

STEP 4

STEP 5

STEP 6

STEP 7

STEP 8

The next few pages introduce some simple tunes using everything you have learned so far.

To make the tunes more interesting we need to know how long to hold a note down for. We will be learning about all the different notes, their names and their lengths soon.

Do not worry too much about timing and rhythm at the moment – this section is all about **practising** the **notes**.

FREE ACCESS on smartphones, iPhone, Android etc. Use any QR code app to scan this QR code

Or go straight to www.flametreemusic.com to **HEAR** chords, scales, and find more resources

We will use two types of note, a short note and a long note:

Short Note

crotchet

Long Note

minim

Try all these tunes at different speeds to find the version you like most.

FREE ACCESS on smartphones, iPhone, Android etc.
Use any QR code app to scan this QR code

Or go straight to www.flametreemusic.com to
HEAR chords, scales, and find more resources

STEP
1

STEP
2

STEP
3

STEP
4

STEP
5

STEP
6

STEP
7

STEP
8

Right Hand Tune

Mouse Dance

Starts with middle finger on E

FREE ACCESS on smartphones, iPhone, Android etc.
Use any QR code app to scan this QR code

Or go straight to www.flametreemusic.com to
HEAR chords, scales, and find more resources

88

Left Hand Tune

Elephant Dance

Starts with little finger on G

STEP 1

STEP 2

STEP 3

STEP 4

STEP 5

STEP 6

STEP 7

STEP 8

FREE ACCESS on smartphones, iPhone, Android etc.
Use any QR code app to scan this QR code

Or go straight to www.flametreemusic.com to
HEAR chords, scales, and find more resources

Right Hand Again

Crocodile Dance

You will need to jump around in this one

Left Hand Again

Snake Dance

You will need to jump around in this one too

STEP 1

STEP 2

STEP 3

STEP 4

STEP 5

STEP 6

STEP 7

STEP 8

STEP 3

RHYTHM & NOTES

Now that we have learned about the pitches
of the notes, we need to think about the rhythm.
Music is not lots of notes all of the same length;
listen to any tune and you will hear fast, slow,
long and short notes.

Rhythm is not about pure speed, it is all
to do with how long notes are in comparison
to all the others around it.

**STEP
1**

**STEP
2**

**STEP
3**

**STEP
4**

**STEP
5**

**STEP
6**

**STEP
7**

**STEP
8**

FREE ACCESS on smartphones, iPhone, Android etc.
Use any QR code app to scan this QR code

Or go straight to www.flametreemusic.com to
HEAR chords, scales, and find more resources

STEP
1

STEP
2

STEP
3

STEP
4

STEP
5

STEP
6

STEP
7

STEP
8

Keeping a Steady Pulse

Most music has a steady pulse. You need to keep this pulse going whilst you play the music.

All notes have lengths which are related to the pulse.

Think of a clock ticking – this is a steady pulse. A metronome will provide you with a steady pulse, and you can set this to a wide variety of speeds. Try setting your

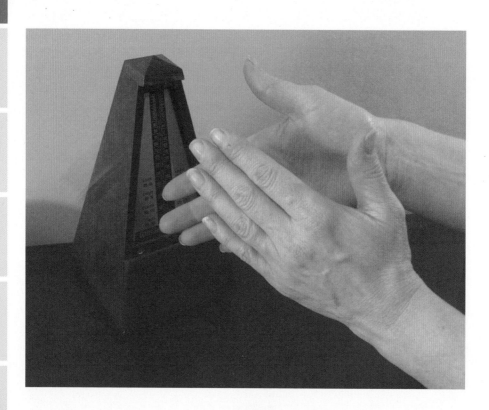

FREE ACCESS on smartphones, iPhone, Android etc.
Use any QR code app to scan this QR code

Or go straight to www.flametreemusic.com to
HEAR chords, scales, and find more resources

94

STEP
1

STEP
2

STEP
3

STEP
4

STEP
5

STEP
6

STEP
7

STEP
8

metronome going then clapping along with it. Make sure your clap is exactly at the same time as the metronome's click, not just after it.

A good sense of rhythm is important. It makes your playing much more musical and enjoyable to listen to. And it is essential if you want to play along with others.

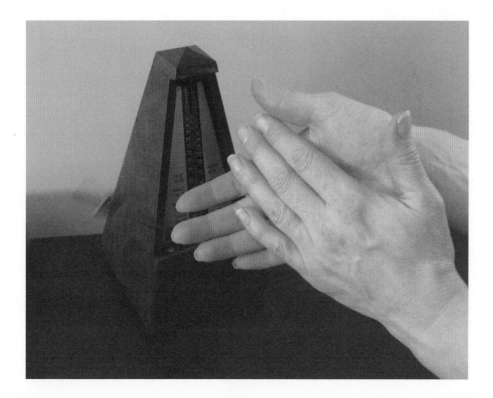

FREE ACCESS on smartphones, iPhone, Android etc. Use any QR code app to scan this QR code

Or go straight to www.flametreemusic.com to **HEAR** chords, scales, and find more resources

95

STEP 1

STEP 2

STEP 3

STEP 4

STEP 5

STEP 6

STEP 7

STEP 8

Try these exercises:

1. With your **left hand**, tap a steady pulse on the table top. Use a metronome to help if necessary.

2. Now, whilst your left hand continues as the same speed, **tap** with your **right hand** in the following ways:

   - Both hands tapping at exactly the same time

   - Right hand taps exactly twice as fast as the left

   - Right hand taps between the left hand taps

3. Now try **reversing** the hands over, so the right hand has the main beat.

Here are a few more complicated rhythms:

For each of them, the left hand should keep a steady pulse whilst the right hand fits in. Again, try swapping the hands over when you have got the hang of it.

The red dots should be the loudest.

Accented beat.

Standard beat.

FREE ACCESS on smartphones, iPhone, Android etc. Use any QR code app to scan this QR code

Or go straight to www.flametreemusic.com to **HEAR** chords, scales, and find more resources

96

RH:

LH:

RH:

LH:

RH:

LH:

RH:

LH:

RH:

LH:

RH:

LH:

STEP
1

STEP
2

STEP
3

STEP
4

STEP
5

STEP
6

STEP
7

STEP
8

FREE ACCESS on smartphones, iPhone, Android etc.
Use any QR code app to scan this QR code

Or go straight to www.flametreemusic.com to
HEAR chords, scales, and find more resources

Note Values

All notes have a length or value – often referred to as how many counts they last for.

Most of the time we use the **quarter note** (**crotchet**) as the basis for counting – this note is introduced shortly.

A **quarter note** (**crotchet**) lasts for **one count** and other notes are said to be 2 counts, 4 counts, half a count, etc.

To begin with we will just learn the four most important note values – these will be sufficient to play a lot of different tunes.

An important thing to remember is that all bars should be filled up – if your music has a **pulse** 'in 4' then you will need note values totaling 4 in every bar.

A single 4-count note or two 2-count notes for example.

FREE ACCESS on smartphones, iPhone, Android etc. Use any QR code app to scan this QR code   Or go straight to www.flametreemusic.com to **HEAR** chords, scales, and find more resources

There are two naming systems for the notes; choose which one you prefer.

American, **jazz** and **popular** terminology tends to prefer names like **whole note**, **quarter note**, etc.

Classical music uses words such as **semibreve**, **crotchet**, etc.

STEP 1
STEP 2
STEP 3
STEP 4
STEP 5
STEP 6
STEP 7
STEP 8

Whole note/Semibreve

A **whole note** (**semibreve**) lasts for **4 counts**. It **fills** a standard **bar**, hence the name 'whole note'.

Here are a few bars of whole notes (semibreves).

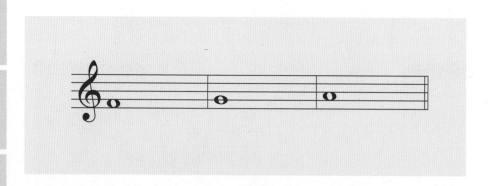

FREE ACCESS on smartphones, iPhone, Android etc.
Use any QR code app to scan this QR code

Or go straight to www.flametreemusic.com to
HEAR chords, scales, and find more resources

100

Half Note/Minim

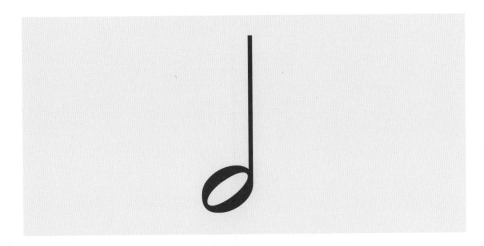

A **half note (minim)** lasts for **2 counts**. You need two of these to fill a standard bar. A **half note** (**minim**) is **half** the length of a **whole note (semibreve)**.

Here are a few bars of half notes (minims).

STEP 1

STEP 2

STEP 3

STEP 4

STEP 5

STEP 6

STEP 7

STEP 8

STEP
1

STEP
2

STEP
3

STEP
4

STEP
5

STEP
6

STEP
7

STEP
8

Quarter Note/Crotchet

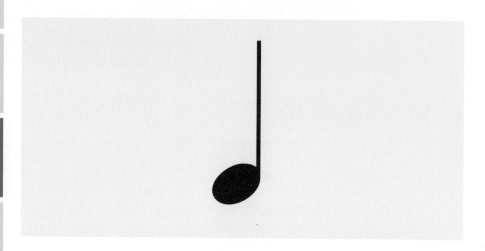

A **quarter note (crotchet)** lasts for **1 count**. You need **four** of these to **fill** a standard **bar**. A quarter note (crotchet) is **half** the length of a **half note** (minim).

Here are a few bars of quarter notes (crotchets).

Eighth Note/Quaver

A **single eighth note (quaver)** looks slightly different when written on its own and when there are several written together. When written together, their tails join together to make a beam.

An **eighth note (quaver)** lasts for **half** a count. You need **eight** of these to **fill** a standard **bar**. An eighth note (quaver) is **half** the length of a **quarter note (crotchet)**.

Quavers are often grouped together in twos or fours. Here are a few bars of eighth notes (quavers).

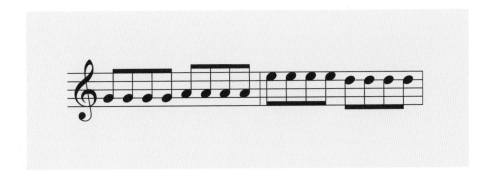

FREE ACCESS on smartphones, iPhone, Android etc. Use any QR code app to scan this QR code

Or go straight to www.flametreemusic.com to **HEAR** chords, scales, and find more resources

STEP 1

STEP 2

STEP 3

STEP 4

STEP 5

STEP 6

STEP 7

STEP 8

STEP
1

STEP
2

STEP
3

STEP
4

STEP
5

STEP
6

STEP
7

STEP
8

Rests

As was mentioned in the section about notes, a bar needs to be filled – you cannot leave a gap.

So what do we do when we want a silence in the music?

This is where rests come in – they are actually place holders for silent beats. This way, you will know exactly how long to wait before playing the next note.

For **every note** there is an **equivalent rest**.

We have just learned four common notes, now let's meet the four rests.

We will see some examples of:

whole note rest
half note rest
quarter note rest
eighth note rest.

The **alternative** terms for these are

semibreve rest
minim rest
crotchet rest
quaver rest.

STEP
1

STEP
2

STEP
3

STEP
4

STEP
5

STEP
6

STEP
7

STEP
8

FREE ACCESS on smartphones, iPhone, Android etc.
Use any QR code app to scan this QR code

Or go straight to www.flametreemusic.com to
HEAR chords, scales, and find more resources

STEP
1

STEP
2

STEP
3

STEP
4

STEP
5

STEP
6

STEP
7

STEP
8

Whole Note Rest/Semibreve Rest

A whole note rest (semibreve rest) lasts for **4 counts**.

The whole note rest is also used to indicate **a whole bar rest** – so if we have bars which are only 3 beats long, this rest will actually last for three beats in this case.

Half Note Rest/Minim Rest

A half note rest (minim rest) lasts for **2 counts**.

You need **two** of these to **fill a standard bar**.

A half note rest (minim rest) is half the length of a whole note rest (semibreve rest).

FREE ACCESS on smartphones, iPhone, Android etc.
Use any QR code app to scan this QR code

Or go straight to www.flametreemusic.com to
HEAR chords, scales, and find more resources

Quarter Note Rest/Crotchet Rest

A quarter note rest (crotchet rest) lasts for **1 count**.

You need four of these to fill a standard bar.

A quarter note rest (crotchet rest) is half the length of a half note rest (minim rest).

Eighth Note Rest/Quaver Rest

An eighth note rest (quaver rest) lasts for **half a count**.

An eighth note rest (quaver rest) is half the length of a quarter note rest (crotchet rest).

You will not normally see a lot of these together – if you need two eighth note rests (quaver rests) together then you would often write a quarter note rest (crotchet rest).

STEP
1

STEP
2

STEP
3

STEP
4

STEP
5

STEP
6

STEP
7

STEP
8

Here a some tunes using rests. Remember to hold the notes down for their full length.

Rest A While

Bouncing Tops

Remember also to make sure there is silence for the length of the rests.

Copy Cat

Waiting Tune

STEP 1

STEP 2

STEP 3

STEP 4

STEP 5

STEP 6

STEP 7

STEP 8

Ties

STEP 1
STEP 2
STEP 3
STEP 4
STEP 5
STEP 6
STEP 7
STEP 8

Some times we need a note to last longer than a standard note length or maybe even longer than a whole bar. We can increase the length of a note by tying two notes together. The symbol used is a curved line which joins the note heads and it is called a 'tie'.

To make music readable, there are several rules. We need not worry about these yet, but you will often see two notes tied together instead of one long one.

For very, very long notes (spanning several bars) we can chain all the notes together using ties.

There is no limit to how many notes can be tied together. Just play the first note and hold it down for the combined length of all the notes.

For example, a **half note (minim)** tied to a **quarter note (crotchet)** will last for 3 beats (2 plus 1).

You will never see rests tied together – only notes.

Try this exercise which makes use of ties.

My Bow Tie

STEP 1

STEP 2

STEP 3

STEP 4

STEP 5

STEP 6

STEP 7

STEP 8

Dotted Notes

Another way of increasing the length of a note is to add a dot to it.

A dot has a specific length in relation to the note it is placed after. It lasts for half the length of the note. Therefore a **dot** placed **after** a **half note (minim)**, which would normally last for two beats, will **increase** the length to three beats.

All the equivalent rests can also have dots placed after them, so a dotted half note rest (dotted minim rest) will be 3 beats of silence.

Opposite are some notes both with and without dots, so you can see the lengths.

STEP 1

STEP 2

STEP 3

STEP 4

STEP 5

STEP 6

STEP 7

STEP 8

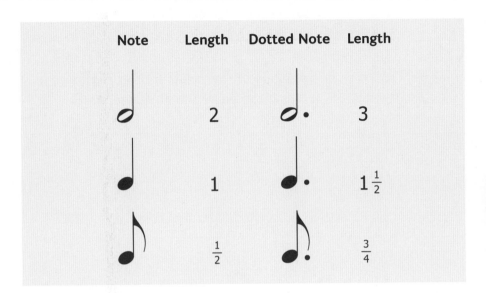

Note	Length	Dotted Note	Length
	2		3
	1		$1\frac{1}{2}$
	$\frac{1}{2}$		$\frac{3}{4}$

Try this exercise which makes use of dotted notes.

Spotty Dotty

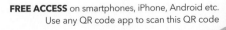

Or go straight to www.flametreemusic.com to **HEAR** chords, scales, and find more resources

STEP 1

STEP 2

STEP 3

STEP 4

STEP 5

STEP 6

STEP 7

STEP 8

Time Signatures

So far we have been using bars with four beats in. This need not be the case for all tunes. Music can be in one of several time signatures.

A time signature consists of two numbers.

- The **top** number tells you how many beats there are in each bar.

- The **bottom** number tells you what sort of beat to use:

  - a **2** stands for **half notes (minims)**

  - a **4** stands for **quarter notes (crotchets)**

  - an **8** stands for **eighth notes (quavers)**.

All the music we have been playing so far has been four quarter notes (crotchets) in each bar – this time signature will have a figure 4 on the top and a 4 on the bottom.

The following pages introduce four of the most common time signatures:

$$\frac{4}{4} \qquad \frac{3}{4} \qquad \frac{2}{4} \qquad \frac{6}{8}$$

FREE ACCESS on smartphones, iPhone, Android etc. Use any QR code app to scan this QR code

Or go straight to www.flametreemusic.com to **HEAR** chords, scales, and find more resources

STEP 1

STEP 2

STEP 3

STEP 4

STEP 5

STEP 6

STEP 7

STEP 8

FREE ACCESS on smartphones, iPhone, Android etc. Use any QR code app to scan this QR code

Or go straight to www.flametreemusic.com to **HEAR** chords, scales, and find more resources

STEP
1

STEP
2

STEP
3

STEP
4

STEP
5

STEP
6

STEP
7

STEP
8

Four quarter notes (crotchets) per bar.

Here is a bar filled with quarter notes (crotchets):

Now try this tune in 4/4 which uses several different note types.

Round About 4

FREE ACCESS on smartphones, iPhone, Android etc.
Use any QR code app to scan this QR code

Or go straight to www.flametreemusic.com to
HEAR chords, scales, and find more resources

116

Three quarter notes (crotchets) per bar.

Here is a bar filled with quarter notes (crotchets):

STEP 1
STEP 2
STEP 3
STEP 4
STEP 5
STEP 6
STEP 7
STEP 8

Now try this tune in 3/4 which uses several different note types.

Three For Tea

FREE ACCESS on smartphones, iPhone, Android etc.
Use any QR code app to scan this QR code

Or go straight to www.flametreemusic.com to
HEAR chords, scales, and find more resources

117

Two quarter notes (crotchets) per bar.

Here is a bar filled with quarter notes (crotchets)

Now try this tune in 2/4 which uses several different note types:

Two's Company

6/8 Six eighth notes (quavers) per bar.

Below is a bar with eighth notes (quavers). See that in 6/8 the eighth notes (quavers) are grouped in threes.

Now try this tune in 6/8 which uses several different note types. Dotted quarter notes (crotchets) are common in 6/8.

Run Around Six

STEP 1
STEP 2
STEP 3
STEP 4
STEP 5
STEP 6
STEP 7
STEP 8

FREE ACCESS on smartphones, iPhone, Android etc. Use any QR code app to scan this QR code

Or go straight to www.flametreemusic.com to **HEAR** chords, scales, and find more resources

STEP
1

STEP
2

STEP
3

STEP
4

STEP
5

STEP
6

STEP
7

STEP
8

What We Know So Far

This section has been all about rhythm.

1. Rhythm is all about the relationship of notes to a regular **pulse**.

2. Different note types have different **lengths**, and every note has an equivalent rest.

3. Both notes and rests can increase their length by half with a **dot** placed after the note or rest.

4. Notes can also be made longer by **tying** together two or more notes.

5. **Time signature**s tell you how many **beats** are in each bar, and what sort of beat they are.

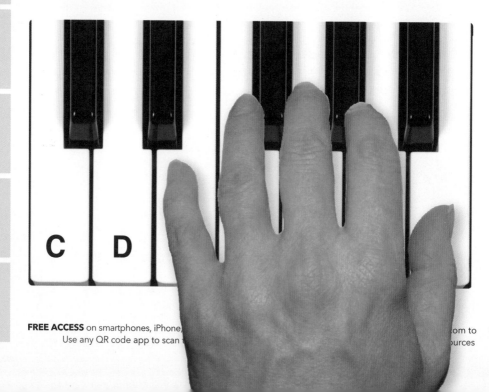

FREE ACCESS on smartphones, iPhone, ...om to
Use any QR code app to scan ... ources

Now Try This

The tunes on the next pages pull together all you have learned in this section.

1. Remember to keep a **steady pulse** all the way through.

2. You will find that putting a little **emphasis** on the **first note** in **every bar** will help you keep a steady rhythm.

3. Do not play too fast – it is more important to **keep a steady pulse**.

4. **The left hand** in some of these exercises is **used** to help **keep** the **rhythm steady** – with notes just on the main beats of the bar, which are usually the first beat and sometimes the middle beat of each bar.

5. **Practise each tune hands separately** at first so you can see what each hand is doing, then try putting the hands together.

6. **Use a metronome** to help you keep the pulse steady – a setting between 60 and 80 will work well for these tunes.

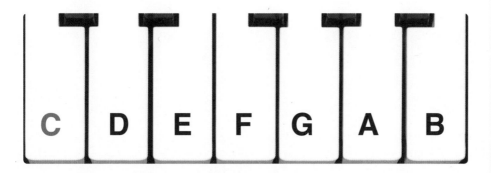

STEP 1
STEP 2
STEP 3
STEP 4
STEP 5
STEP 6
STEP 7
STEP 8

FREE ACCESS on smartphones, iPhone, Android etc. Use any QR code app to scan this QR code

Or go straight to www.flametreemusic.com to **HEAR** chords, scales, and find more resources

Three Blind Mice

Tea Pot Twirl

This Old Man

STEP
1

STEP
2

STEP
3

STEP
4

STEP
5

STEP
6

STEP
7

STEP
8

FREE ACCESS on smartphones, iPhone, Android etc. Use any QR code app to scan this QR code

Or go straight to www.flametreemusic.com to **HEAR** chords, scales, and find more resources

STEP 1

STEP 2

STEP 3

STEP 4

STEP 5

STEP 6

STEP 7

STEP 8

Mitzi's Waltz

Royal Tune

Syncopated Twos

Copy Cat Bounce

FREE ACCESS on smartphones, iPhone, Android etc. Use any QR code app to scan this QR code

Or go straight to www.flametreemusic.com to **HEAR** chords, scales, and find more resources

STEP 1

STEP 2

STEP 3

STEP 4

STEP 5

STEP 6

STEP 7

STEP 8

Pop Goes The Weasel

any high note

Or go straight to www.flametreemusic.com to **HEAR** chords, scales, and find more resources

Jack and Jill

STEP
1

STEP
2

STEP
3

STEP
4

STEP
5

STEP
6

STEP
7

STEP
8

STEP 4

SCALES & ACCIDENTALS

We have covered all the white notes and you have started to try out the black notes. We have also covered note lengths and rhythm. Now we move on to scales and key signatures. Scales are just a row of notes following a set pattern. We will just consider two of these – major scale and harmonic minor scale. You can start a scale on any note on the keyboard, but depending on where you start you will need to use some black notes to make the scale sound correct. This is where key signatures come in.

STEP 1

STEP 2

STEP 3

STEP 4

STEP 5

STEP 6

STEP 7

STEP 8

Hands Together

Before we get in to adding sharps and flats, it would be a good idea to practise playing with the hands together. The left hand is sometimes used to accompany the tune in the right hand and sometimes it has tunes of its own.

On this page you will see a reminder about which finger has which number. The tunes that follow will have some fingering on them to help you put your hand in the correct place.

STEP
1

STEP
2

STEP
3

STEP
4

STEP
5

STEP
6

STEP
7

STEP
8

C   D   E   F   G   A   B

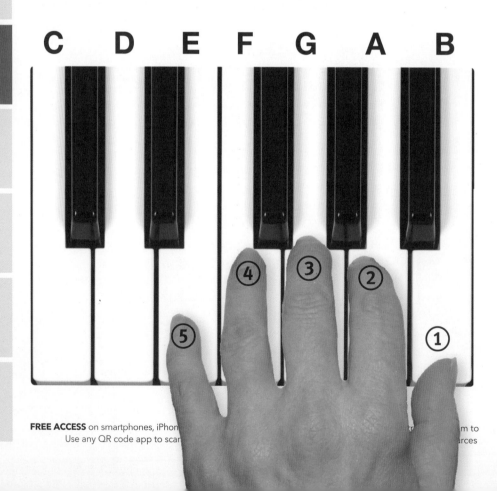

As always with hands-together music, you should learn each hand on its own first. The tunes will not involve moving the hands too often and too far, but we will get more adventurous as we progress.

The first four of the following tunes have been adapted from piano pieces by Schumann – a classical composer who lived in the early nineteenth century. The second group are all from Mozart, who lived in the second half of the eighteenth century.

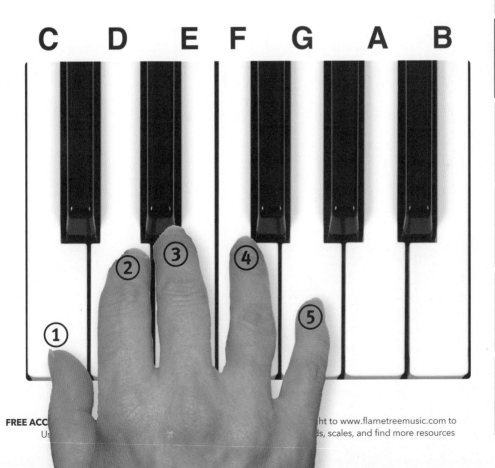

STEP 1

STEP 2

STEP 3

STEP 4

STEP 5

STEP 6

STEP 7

STEP 8

Soldier's Song

Stretch down with
your thumb here

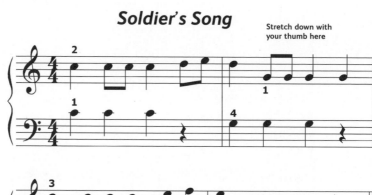

Caprice

FREE ACCESS on smartphones, iPhone, Android etc.
Use any QR code app to scan this QR code

Or go straight to www.flametreemusic.com to
HEAR chords, scales, and find more resources

Slumber Song

Study

STEP 1

STEP 2

STEP 3

STEP 4

STEP 5

STEP 6

STEP 7

STEP 8

Twinkle Twinkle

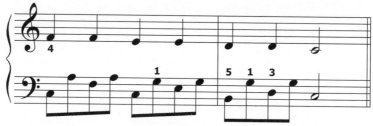

Rondo

Or go straight to www.flametreemusic.com to **HEAR** chords, scales, and find more resources

Allegro 1

Allegro 2

STEP 1
STEP 2
STEP 3
STEP 4
STEP 5
STEP 6
STEP 7
STEP 8

Key Signatures

Key signature is the name given to the collection of sharps or flats at the start of the music. A key signature will consist of just sharps or just flats, you will not get a mixture of both.

Every note on the piano **has a sharp** and a **flat** version, but we will only concern ourselves with key signatures of just one or two sharps or flats for this section.

If there are **no sharps** or **flats** at the start of the music then this too is a key signature – it is the key signature of **C major** and **A minor**.

All the tunes you have played so far have had a C major key signature.

Tunes in C major just use the white notes on the piano – we are now going to venture into using **black notes** in our tunes.

STEP 1

STEP 2

STEP 3

STEP 4

STEP 5

STEP 6

STEP 7

STEP 8

STEP 1

STEP 2

STEP 3

STEP 4

STEP 5

STEP 6

STEP 7

STEP 8

G major

This is a G major key signature.

It has one sharp:
F sharp.

D major

This is a D major key signature.

It has two sharps:
F sharp and **C sharp.**

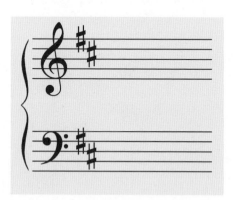

FREE ACCESS on smartphones, iPhone, Android etc. Use any QR code app to scan this QR code

Or go straight to www.flametreemusic.com to **HEAR** chords, scales, and find more resources

138

F major

This is an F major key signature.

It has one flat:
B flat.

B flat major

This is a B flat major key signature.

It has two flats:
B flat and **E flat.**

On the next page there are some tunes using our new key signatures.

STEP 1

STEP 2

STEP 3

STEP 4

STEP 5

STEP 6

STEP 7

STEP 8

Or go straight to www.flametreemusic.com to **HEAR** chords, scales, and find more resources

Waltz in G

D Major Bounce

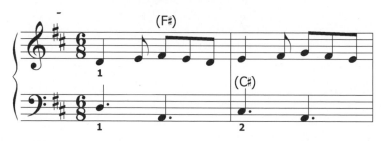

Fun in F

B Flat Ballad

FREE ACCESS on smartphones, iPhone, Android etc.
Use any QR code app to scan this QR code

Or go straight to www.flametreemusic.com to
HEAR chords, scales, and find more resources

Accidentals

Sometimes we need to make a note sharp or flat temporarily. This is where accidentals come in.

If you put an **accidental** sharp in **front** of **a note**, that note will change to a sharp and will stay as a sharp for the rest of the bar. As soon as you get to the **next bar** the note will **revert** back to what it was.

Accidentals can be **sharp**, **flat** or **natural**.

A **sharp** will change a note to the next note **higher** (usually a black note) and a **flat** will change it to the next note **lower**.

A **natural converts** a sharp or flat **back** to the respective white note – you will generally come across naturals when you have music in key signatures with sharps and flats in.

Sharp

This is a sharp sign.

It means play the very next note to the right, which
is usually a black note.

The notes E and B do not have black notes to the right
of them, so their sharps are white notes.

Or go straight to www.flametreemusic.com to
HEAR chords, scales, and find more resources

STEP 1

STEP 2

STEP 3

STEP 4

STEP 5

STEP 6

STEP 7

STEP 8

STEP
1

STEP
2

STEP
3

STEP
4

STEP
5

STEP
6

STEP
7

STEP
8

Flat

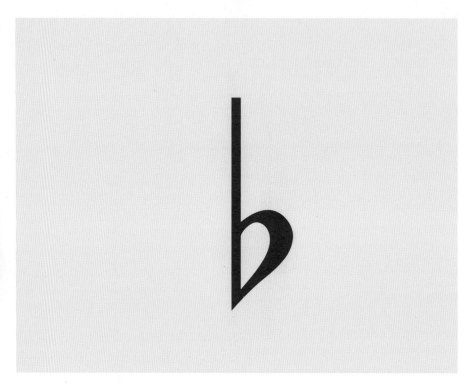

This is a flat sign.

It means play the very next note to the left,
which is usually a black note.

The notes F and C do not have black notes to
the left of them, so their flats are white notes.

FREE ACCESS on smartphones, iPhone, Android etc.
Use any QR code app to scan this QR code

Or go straight to www.flametreemusic.com to
HEAR chords, scales, and find more resources

Natural

This is a natural sign.

It is used to cancel a sharp or flat.

Just play the white note.

STEP 1

STEP 2

STEP 3

STEP 4

STEP 5

STEP 6

STEP 7

STEP 8

STEP
1

STEP
2

STEP
3

STEP
4

STEP
5

STEP
6

STEP
7

STEP
8

Simple Major Scales

You will come across scales, or parts of scales, in many pieces of music.

Look out for rows of notes either going up or going down.

On the opposite page a **C major scale** is shown in both hands, first going up, then going down. Look at the fingering suggested – this makes it easier to play smoothly. (As a reminder, the scale, which uses the white notes only, is also shown below.)

When you need to play the thumb after finger 3, tuck the thumb under to play the next note without a gap. Then, when you are going the other way and need to play '3' after '1', lift finger 3 over the top of the thumb.

Try the tunes on the following pages, all of which include some scale-like passages. See how many scales you can recognize – the first few are pointed out for you.

C D E F G A B

C major scale, going up

Right hand

Left hand

C major scale, going down

Right hand

Left hand

Or go straight to www.flametreemusic.com to
HEAR chords, scales, and find more resources

STEP 1

STEP 2

STEP 3

STEP 4

STEP 5

STEP 6

STEP 7

STEP 8

Little Nut Tree

Chiming Bells

FREE ACCESS on smartphones, iPhone, Android etc.
Use any QR code app to scan this QR code

Or go straight to www.flametreemusic.com to
HEAR chords, scales, and find more resources

Polly Put The Kettle On

STEP 1

STEP 2

STEP 3

STEP 4

STEP 5

STEP 6

STEP 7

STEP 8

Playing By Ear

Remember we learned about playing by ear earlier in the book? You need to listen and create musical shapes in your head.

Here are two tunes with bits missing – try to fill in the gaps with scale-like passages.

You can either copy the shape of the bar before, or mirror what you are given.

You could even play something completely different – as long as it sounds like it fits in with the rest of the music.

Listen carefully to the sound – you may need a few sharps and flats to make it sound right!

STEP 1

STEP 2

STEP 3

STEP 4

STEP 5

STEP 6

STEP 7

STEP 8

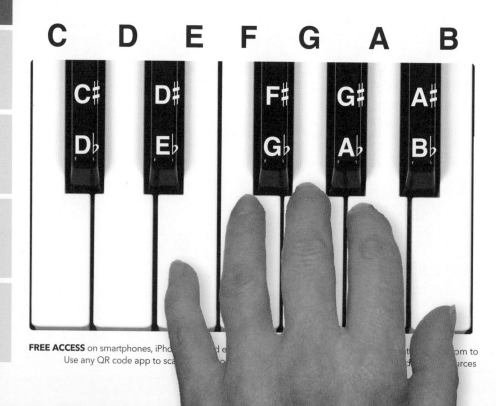

Fill The Gap 1

Fill The Gap 2

STEP 1

STEP 2

STEP 3

STEP 4

STEP 5

STEP 6

STEP 7

STEP 8

STEP
1

STEP
2

STEP
3

STEP
4

STEP
5

STEP
6

STEP
7

STEP
8

What We Know So Far

This section has been all about moving away from just white notes.

1. You have learned all about **sharps**, **flats** and **naturals** – when sharps and flats are collected together at the beginning of the music they are called a **key signature**.

2. Sharps, flats and naturals in front of individual notes are called **accidentals**.

3. Every key signature has a **major scale** and a **minor scale** associated with it. We have learned a few basic ones so far – there are more to come later in the book.

4. Many tunes have **scale-like passages** in them. If you know your scales you will automatically have learned part of almost every tune you will want to play.

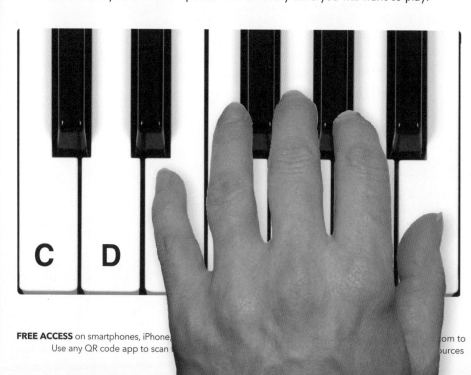

Now Try This

The next few pages combine what we have learned in this section. They are tunes from famous composers which include parts of scales and many other things you have just learned. These tunes also allow you to practise playing in different keys.

Some things to look out for:

Key signature at the start of the music.

Part of a scale going upwards.

Part of a scale going downwards.

Accidentals in the music.

Also watch out for the different types of notes, dotted notes, rests and ties.

FREE ACCESS on smartphones, iPhone, Android etc. Use any QR code app to scan this QR code

Or go straight to www.flametreemusic.com to **HEAR** chords, scales, and find more resources

STEP 1

STEP 2

STEP 3

STEP 4

STEP 5

STEP 6

STEP 7

STEP 8

Melody (Schumann)

STEP 1

STEP 2

STEP 3

STEP 4

STEP 5

STEP 6

STEP 7

STEP 8

Mazurka in C (Chopin)

* This note would be a natural anyway, but an accidental is often
added when you have just played a sharp as a reminder.

STEP 1
STEP 2
STEP 3
STEP 4
STEP 5
STEP 6
STEP 7
STEP 8

Musette (Bach)

Fugue (Pachelbel)

FREE ACCESS on smartphones, iPhone, Android etc.
Use any QR code app to scan this QR code

Or go straight to www.flametreemusic.com to
HEAR chords, scales, and find more resources

157

STEP 1

STEP 2

STEP 3

STEP 4

STEP 5

STEP 6

STEP 7

STEP 8

STEP 5

INTERVALS & CHORDS

On the piano, you can play several notes at the same time. The distance between two notes is referred to as the 'interval' between them. When you have three or more notes, this is called a chord. Any group of notes could be called a chord, but some sound much better than others. The best-sounding ones consist of three notes which are each just separated by one note on the keyboard.

In this section we will look in more detail at chords and intervals.

STEP 1
STEP 2
STEP 3
STEP 4
STEP 5
STEP 6
STEP 7
STEP 8

Intervals

An interval is the distance between two notes. You count the lowest notes as '1' then count up through the letter names until you reach the higher note.

The easiest way to see how this works is to use the **C major scale** and see how far each note of the scale is from the starting note.

C to D is just 1 step,

so C = 1 then D = 2.

It is called a second.

C to E is two steps up,

so C = 1, D = 2 and E = 3.

It is called a third.

Look at the chart opposite. This shows you all the main intervals in the keys of **C major** and **G major**.

FREE ACCESS on smartphones, iPhone, Android etc.
Use any QR code app to scan this QR code

Or go straight to www.flametreemusic.com to
HEAR chords, scales, and find more resources

STEP 1
STEP 2
STEP 3
STEP 4
STEP 5
STEP 6
STEP 7
STEP 8

Intervals in C major

Right Hand

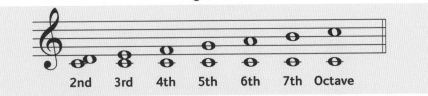

2nd   3rd   4th   5th   6th   7th   Octave

Left Hand

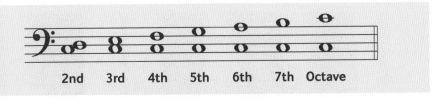

2nd   3rd   4th   5th   6th   7th   Octave

Intervals in G major

Right Hand

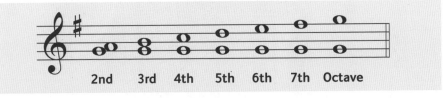

2nd   3rd   4th   5th   6th   7th   Octave

Left Hand

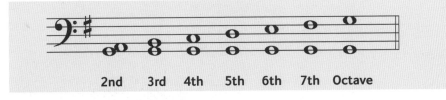

2nd   3rd   4th   5th   6th   7th   Octave

STEP 1
STEP 2
STEP 3
STEP 4
STEP 5
STEP 6
STEP 7
STEP 8

FREE ACCESS on smartphones, iPhone, Android etc.
Use any QR code app to scan this QR code

Or go straight to www.flametreemusic.com to
HEAR chords, scales, and find more resources

STEP
1

STEP
2

STEP
3

STEP
4

STEP
5

STEP
6

STEP
7

STEP
8

Exercises

Here are a few exercises using intervals.

Intervals can be written with the notes together (known as a **harmonic interval**) or with the notes one after the other (known as a **melodic interval**).

These exercises use both – look carefully and you will see the difference between harmonic intervals and melodic intervals.

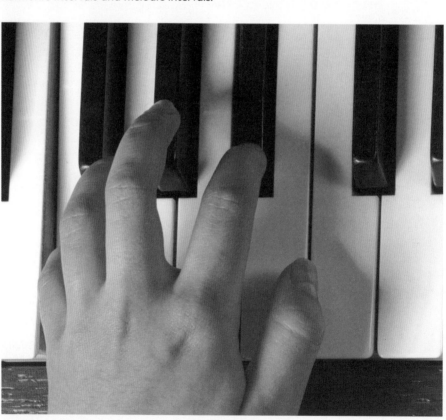

Jumping in Three

Chorale (Schumann)

STEP
1

STEP
2

STEP
3

STEP
4

STEP
5

STEP
6

STEP
7

STEP
8

FREE ACCESS on smartphones, iPhone, Android etc. Use any QR code app to scan this QR code Or go straight to www.flametreemusic.com to **HEAR** chords, scales, and find more resources

STEP 1

STEP 2

STEP 3

STEP 4

STEP 5

STEP 6

STEP 7

STEP 8

Study (Czerny)

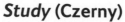

Rambling Brook

Study in 6ths (Czerny)

STEP
1

STEP
2

STEP
3

STEP
4

STEP
5

STEP
6

STEP
7

STEP
8

Simple Chords

Here are some simple 3-note chords, based just on the white notes.

Listen carefully and see if you can hear the **difference** between **major** and **minor** chords – generally, **major** chords are **brighter** and **minor** chords sound more **solemn**.

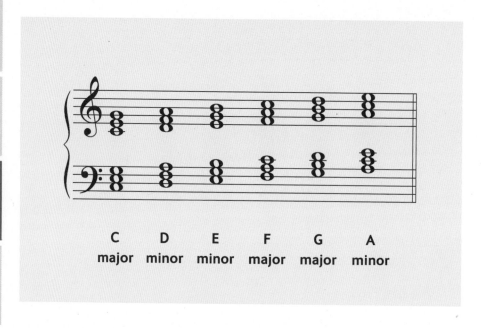

The **chords** so far have been in '**root**' position.

This means that the **lowest note** of the chord is the one which gives it its name, so **C major** starts on its root note C, **G major** starts on its root G and **A minor** starts on the root note A.

Or go straight to www.flametreemusic.com to **HEAR** chords, scales, and find more resources

We can play the same notes in a different order to get '**inverted**' chords.

Here are a few:

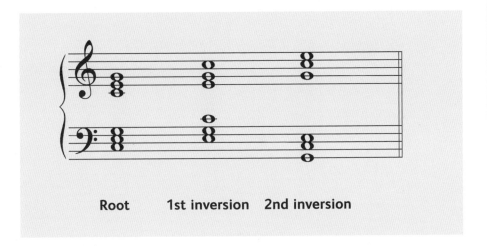

The next two pages have some simple chord exercises so you can get used to playing them.

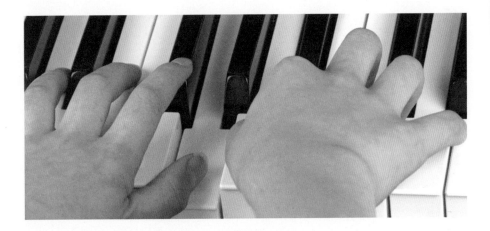

FREE ACCESS on smartphones, iPhone, Android etc. Use any QR code app to scan this QR code

Or go straight to www.flametreemusic.com to **HEAR** chords, scales, and find more resources

167

STEP 1

STEP 2

STEP 3

STEP 4

STEP 5

STEP 6

STEP 7

STEP 8

Chords 1

Chords 2

Or go straight to www.flametreemusic.com to
HEAR chords, scales, and find more resources

Chords 3

Chords 4

Or go straight to www.flametreemusic.com to
HEAR chords, scales, and find more resources

STEP
1

STEP
2

STEP
3

STEP
4

STEP
5

STEP
6

STEP
7

STEP
8

Here are two simple tunes with just the **right hand** written out. Listen carefully to the music then try to **add** some **simple chords** in the **left hand** (one per bar).

Keep to 'root position' chords to begin with as these are easier to play. Remember to include sharps or flats if they are shown in the key signature.

The tunes which follow these are based on **intervals** and **chords**.

By the way, do you remember seeing and playing middle C? It was pointed out quite early on in this book. If you look at the note you will see it has a little line of its own – this is called a ledger line. When you need notes higher or lower than would fit on the staff, you use ledger lines. Here are a few notes on ledger lines:

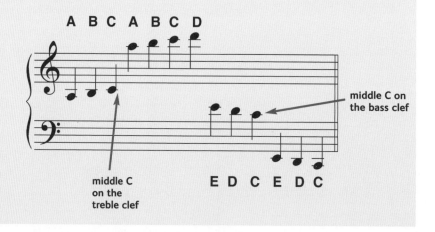

A B C A B C D

middle C on the bass clef

middle C on the treble clef

E D C E D C

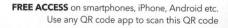
FREE ACCESS on smartphones, iPhone, Android etc.
Use any QR code app to scan this QR code

Or go straight to www.flametreemusic.com to
HEAR chords, scales, and find more resources

170

Find The Chords 1

Find The Chords 2

STEP 1
STEP 2
STEP 3
STEP 4
STEP 5
STEP 6
STEP 7
STEP 8

Country Dance (Beethoven)

FREE ACCESS on smartphones, iPhone, Android etc.
Use any QR code app to scan this QR code

Or go straight to www.flametreemusic.com to
HEAR chords, scales, and find more resources

Sonatina (Beethoven)

STEP 1

STEP 2

STEP 3

STEP 4

STEP 5

STEP 6

STEP 7

STEP 8

What We Know So Far

This chapter has been all about intervals and chords.

1. The distance between two notes is called an **interval**.

2. **The size of an interval is the** number of notes from the lowest to the highest, counting the starting note as 1.

3. Intervals can be played as **separate** notes one after the other or played **together**.

4. A **chord** is a group of notes played together.

5. The most common chords are either **major** or **minor**.

6. Chords are named after the **lowest** note, when played in **root** position.

7. **Chords** are a common way of **accompanying** a melody.

8. Not all instruments can play chords. A **piano** and a **guitar** can, but brass or wind instruments, such as a trumpet or clarinet, can not.

FREE ACCESS on smartphones, iPhone, Android etc.
Use any QR code app to scan this QR code

Or go straight to www.flametreemusic.com to
HEAR chords, scales, and find more resources

174

Now Try This

Music with intervals and chords

The music on the next few pages will help you practise playing chords. You can also go to the Flame Tree Red Book in the Pieces section online at FlameTreeMusic.com, to find more sheet music.

Sometimes a chord is not played with all the notes at once but one after the other. You have already met this type of accompaniment in previous sections. Look back at some of the pieces by Mozart you have played and see if you can spot the **'broken' chords**.

It is often the left hand that plays **chords**, but the right hand can play them as well. As you listen to music, decide whether it is a simple melody with a chordal accompaniment or both hands are playing chords.

There is a specific type of 'broken' chord called an **arpeggio**. We will learn about these soon.

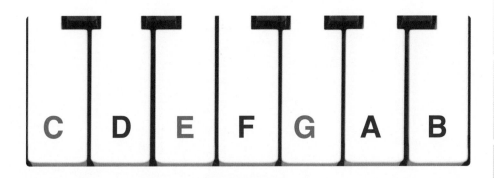

FREE ACCESS on smartphones, iPhone, Android etc.
Use any QR code app to scan this QR code

Or go straight to www.flametreemusic.com to
HEAR chords, scales, and find more resources

STEP 1
STEP 2
STEP 3
STEP 4
STEP 5
STEP 6
STEP 7
STEP 8

Presto (Mozart)

Presto (Haydn)

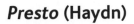

STEP
1

STEP
2

STEP
3

STEP
4

STEP
5

STEP
6

STEP
7

STEP
8

STEP 1
STEP 2
STEP 3
STEP 4
STEP 5
STEP 6
STEP 7
STEP 8

Largo (Handel)

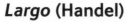

Italian Song (Tchaikovsky)

STEP
1

STEP
2

STEP
3

STEP
4

**STEP
5**

STEP
6

STEP
7

STEP
8

Or go straight to www.flametreemusic.com to
HEAR chords, scales, and find more resources

STEP 6

ARPEGGIOS

Chords have been introduced to show you how to play several notes together. We now show you another use of this knowledge of chords. When all the notes of a chord are played together it is just called a 'chord', but when you play the notes of a chord one by one it is known as a 'broken chord'.

This section covers broken chords and also a more 'formal' version of the broken chord – an 'arpeggio'.

STEP
1

STEP
2

STEP
3

STEP
4

STEP
5

STEP
6

STEP
7

STEP
8

Moving Around The Keyboard

Scales help you move around the keyboard note by note, but broken chords and arpeggios help you move around in larger steps.

The exercises on the following two pages show you ways of moving around the keyboard using arpeggios. Take note of the fingering – as in the scales, the thumb should be tucked under the fingers to reach the next note to make all the notes smooth and avoid gaps in the sound.

Broken chords are also a very effective way of creating a moving accompaniment rather than a static one. Look back at some of the music you have just learned.

Here are some examples of broken chords:

Here's another note you need to know:

It is a sixteenth note (semiquaver). It is **half** the length of an **eighth note (quaver)**, so you will need 16 of them to fill a standard bar. Sixteenth notes are often written in groups of 4. Here is a 4/4 bar full of sixteenth notes.

FREE ACCESS on smartphones, iPhone, Android etc. Use any QR code app to scan this QR code

Or go straight to www.flametreemusic.com to **HEAR** chords, scales, and find more resources

C major chord

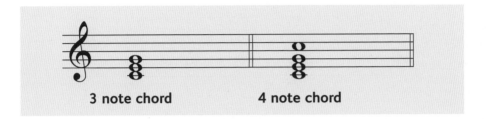

3 note chord   **4 note chord**

Broken chord using 3 notes

Broken chord using 4 notes

Now try the exercises overleaf to practise arpeggios.

STEP 1

STEP 2

STEP 3

STEP 4

STEP 5

STEP 6

STEP 7

STEP 8

STEP 1

STEP 2

STEP 3

STEP 4

STEP 5

STEP 6

STEP 7

STEP 8

Arpeggio Exercise 1

Arpeggio Exercise 2

Arpeggio Melody

STEP
1

STEP
2

STEP
3

STEP
4

STEP
5

STEP
6

STEP
7

STEP
8

STEP
1

STEP
2

STEP
3

STEP
4

STEP
5

STEP
6

STEP
7

STEP
8

Simple Broken Chords

The word 'arpeggio' refers to a more formal playing of the broken chord in that all the notes of the chord should be played in order.

A broken chord is simply the notes of the chord 'broken up' into single notes played one after the other.

Here are two simple examples, one of a broken chord pattern and one of an arpeggio pattern. Both based on the C major chord.

FREE ACCESS on smartphones, iPhone, Android etc. Use any QR code app to scan this QR code

Or go straight to www.flametreemusic.com to **HEAR** chords, scales, and find more resources

Broken chord based on C major

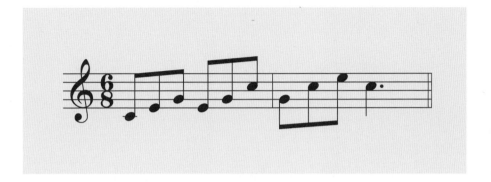

C major arpeggio

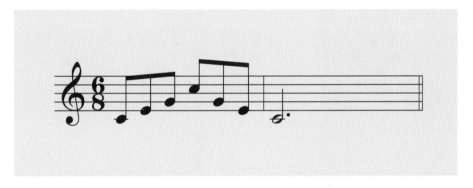

The two tunes that follow are basically the same, but the first uses broken chords and the second uses arpeggios.

On the next few pages are two tunes for you to add your own accompaniment to. Use broken chords and arpeggios. There is just one chord per bar.

STEP 1
STEP 2
STEP 3
STEP 4
STEP 5
STEP 6
STEP 7
STEP 8

Waltz in G (broken chord version)

STEP
1

STEP
2

STEP
3

STEP
4

STEP
5

STEP
6

STEP
7

STEP
8

Waltz in G (arpeggio chord version)

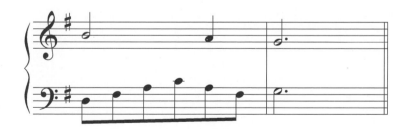

STEP 1

STEP 2

STEP 3

STEP 4

STEP 5

STEP 6

STEP 7

STEP 8

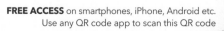

Trumpet Call

Bumping Along

STEP 1
STEP 2
STEP 3
STEP 4
STEP 5
STEP 6
STEP 7
STEP 8

FREE ACCESS on smartphones, iPhone, Android etc. Use any QR code app to scan this QR code

Or go straight to www.flametreemusic.com to **HEAR** chords, scales, and find more resources

STEP 1
STEP 2
STEP 3
STEP 4
STEP 5
STEP 6
STEP 7
STEP 8

What We Know So Far

This section has been all about broken chords and arpeggios. Here are a few things to remember:

1. **Broken chords** are **notes** of a **chord** played **one at a time**.

2. **Arpeggios** are **broken chords**, but with all the notes of the chord **played in order**.

3. **Broken chords** are a common way of creating an **accompaniment** to a tune.

4. **Broken chords** and **arpeggios** are an effective way of **moving around** the **keyboard** without jumping about.

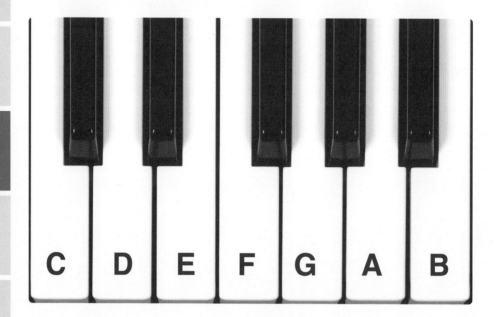

C D E F G A B

FREE ACCESS on smartphones, iPhone, Android etc. Use any QR code app to scan this QR code

Or go straight to www.flametreemusic.com to **HEAR** chords, scales, and find more resources

192

Now Try This

What we need now are some examples of well-known music that uses broken chords and arpeggios.

The following six pages contain music specially chosen to demonstrate this.

Don't forget, broken chords can appear in either hand and can be an accompaniment or an integral part of the melody.

Listen carefully as you play and see if you can spot all the broken chords.

Also see if you can work out what chord is actually being used. To do this, play the notes which you think are part of the broken chord all together.

FREE ACCESS on smartphones, iPhone, Android etc. Use any QR code app to scan this QR code

Or go straight to www.flametreemusic.com to **HEAR** chords, scales, and find more resources

193

STEP 1

STEP 2

STEP 3

STEP 4

STEP 5

STEP 6

STEP 7

STEP 8

Prelude No. 1 (Bach)

STEP 1

STEP 2

STEP 3

STEP 4

STEP 5

STEP 6

STEP 7

STEP 8

Sonatina in G (Diabelli)

FREE ACCESS on smartphones, iPhone, Android etc.
Use any QR code app to scan this QR code

Or go straight to www.flametreemusic.com to
HEAR chords, scales, and find more resources

196

STEP 1

STEP 2

STEP 3

STEP 4

STEP 5

STEP 6

STEP 7

STEP 8

Rondo in G (Bertini)

STEP
1

STEP
2

STEP
3

STEP
4

STEP
5

STEP
6

STEP
7

STEP
8

FREE ACCESS on smartphones, iPhone, Android etc.
Use any QR code app to scan this QR code

Or go straight to www.flametreemusic.com to
HEAR chords, scales, and find more resources

STEP 7

EXPRESSION

We have come a long way now but there is a crucial ingredient missing: expression.

You know what notes to play and how long to hold the notes down for. You also know how long to leave silences for (the rests). You have played scale-like passages, broken chords and jumped around the keyboard.

This chapter is all about how to really *play* the music. We will learn how loud to play, when to play smoothly and when to play short, detached notes, how to use the pedals and how to play 'ornaments'.

STEP 1

STEP 2

STEP 3

STEP 4

STEP 5

STEP 6

STEP 7

STEP 8

FREE ACCESS on smartphones, iPhone, Android etc. Use any QR code app to scan this QR code

Or go straight to www.flametreemusic.com to **HEAR** chords, scales, and find more resources

STEP
1

STEP
2

STEP
3

STEP
4

STEP
5

STEP
6

STEP
7

STEP
8

Dynamics

The word 'dynamics' means the louds and softs when playing the keys.

All the **main musical terms** you will come across in this section are **Italian** words – but don't worry, there are not too many of them.

The chart on the opposite page shows all the common dynamic markings. You will not often come across anything else.

We will follow this with some tunes that include dynamics so you can see how they look in the music.

FREE ACCESS on smartphones, iPhone, Android etc. Use any QR code app to scan this QR code

Or go straight to www.flametreemusic.com to **HEAR** chords, scales, and find more resources

Symbol	Full Term	Meaning
_ff_	_fortissimo_	very loud
_f_	_forte_	loud
_mf_	_mezzoforte_	moderately loud
_mp_	_mezzopiano_	moderately soft
_p_	_piano_	soft
_pp_	_pianissimo_	very soft
<	_crescendo_	gradually louder
>	_decrescendo_	gradually softer

FREE ACCESS on smartphones, iPhone, Android etc.
Use any QR code app to scan this QR code

Or go straight to www.flametreemusic.com to
HEAR chords, scales, and find more resources

La Donna e Mobile (Verdi)

Minuet in G (Böhm)

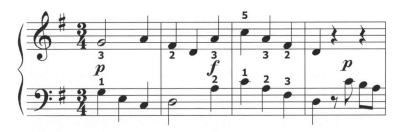

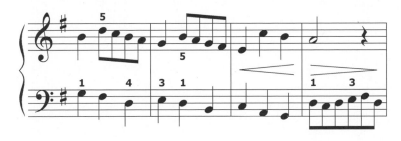

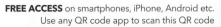

Slurs

Curved lines are used in many places in a piece of music, and they can mean different things. You met one of these a while ago — that was the tie. A tie is a curved line joining two notes of the same pitch.

The curved line we are looking at here is one which **joins** two **different notes**, or it could go across three or more notes. A **slur**, in piano music, means **play** the **notes smoothly** (do not put a gap between the notes).

Here are some examples to show you the **difference** between **ties** and **slurs**. These are followed by some simple tunes with slurs included — make sure there are no gaps during each slur.

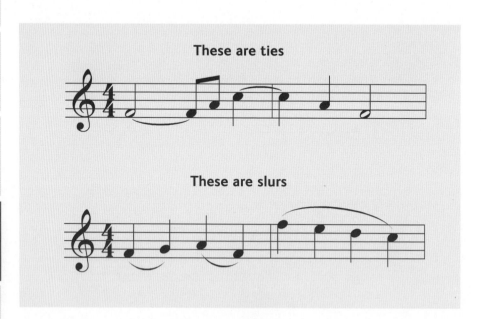

These are ties

These are slurs

FREE ACCESS on smartphones, iPhone, Android etc.
Use any QR code app to scan this QR code

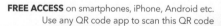

Or go straight to www.flametreemusic.com to
HEAR chords, scales, and find more resources

206

Bow The Lament

Slur's The Word

STEP
1

STEP
2

STEP
3

STEP
4

STEP
5

STEP
6

STEP
7

STEP
8

Or go straight to www.flametreemusic.com to **HEAR** chords, scales, and find more resources

The Mill *Stream* (Múller)

FREE ACCESS on smartphones, iPhone, Android etc.
Use any QR code app to scan this QR code

Or go straight to www.flametreemusic.com to
HEAR chords, scales, and find more resources

208

Minuet in D (Beethoven)

STEP
1

STEP
2

STEP
3

STEP
4

STEP
5

STEP
6

**STEP
7**

STEP
8

FREE ACCESS on smartphones, iPhone, Android etc.
Use any QR code app to scan this QR code

Or go straight to www.flametreemusic.com to
HEAR chords, scales, and find more resources

STEP 1

STEP 2

STEP 3

STEP 4

STEP 5

STEP 6

STEP 7

STEP 8

Staccato and Legato

In music, the opposite to smooth is 'detached'.

We have just learned about slurs, which show where to play smoothly, so now we need to know when to play detached – also called '**staccato**'.

There is a difference between 'leaving a gap' and playing 'staccato' – staccato is usually shorter.

Going back to the slur for a moment – there is another way for a composer to indicate smooth music. If a **whole section** is to be **smooth** and **without gaps** then the term used is '**legato**' – this saves having to put a slur line over everything.

The following exercises demonstrate the **difference** between separate, **legato** and **staccato**. When you understand this, play the tunes on the next page – there is one 'legato' tune and one 'staccato' tune.

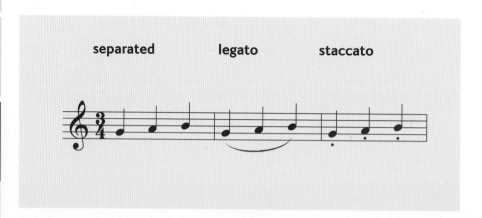

separated   legato   staccato

FREE ACCESS on smartphones, iPhone, Android etc. Use any QR code app to scan this QR code

Or go straight to www.flametreemusic.com to **HEAR** chords, scales, and find more resources

210

Minuet in G (Beethoven)

STEP 1

STEP 2

STEP 3

STEP 4

STEP 5

STEP 6

STEP 7

STEP 8

FREE ACCESS on smartphones, iPhone, Android etc. Use any QR code app to scan this QR code

Or go straight to www.flametreemusic.com to **HEAR** chords, scales, and find more resources

STEP
1

STEP
2

STEP
3

STEP
4

STEP
5

STEP
6

STEP
7

STEP
8

Using Pedals

Most upright pianos have two pedals and most grand pianos have three. We will not worry about the middle pedal for now.

The pedal on the **left** is the **damping pedal** (often called the '**soft pedal**'), and the pedal on the **right** is called the '**sustaining pedal**'.

The **soft pedal** can physically work in a number of different ways, depending on how the piano is manufactured. Here are the three most common ways:

1. The hammers are moved closer to the strings, so they hit them with less force.

2. The hammers are all moved to the right so that notes with multiple strings just use one of them.

3. A piece of felt is raised between the hammers and the string, creating a muted sound.

Look inside your piano and press the pedal to see which technique yours uses.

The **sustaining pedal** simply **raises** the piano's **dampers off** the **strings** to allow any notes played to keep on sounding until they die out.

FREE ACCESS on smartphones, iPhone, Android etc.
Use any QR code app to scan this QR code

Or go straight to www.flametreemusic.com to
HEAR chords, scales, and find more resources

FREE ACCESS on smartphones, iPhone, Android etc. Use any QR code app to scan this QR code

Or go straight to www.flametreemusic.com to **HEAR** chords, scales, and find more resources

STEP 1
STEP 2
STEP 3
STEP 4
STEP 5
STEP 6
STEP 7
STEP 8

STEP
1

STEP
2

STEP
3

STEP
4

STEP
5

STEP
6

STEP
7

STEP
8

The Soft Pedal

The pedal on the left will not automatically make your music soft – you can still play loud with this pedal depressed.

What it does is make it a lot easier to play softly, and will allow you to play much softer than without it.

Try the following tune both with and without the soft pedal – see how quietly you can play without the notes disappearing completely.

Quietly Does It

FREE ACCESS on smartphones, iPhone, Android etc.
Use any QR code app to scan this QR code

Or go straight to www.flametreemusic.com to
HEAR chords, scales, and find more resources

214

The Sustaining Pedal

The marking in the music which tells you to press the sustaining pedal is either a simple 'P' or a swirly 'Ped.' symbol.

You release the pedal where you see a star, or sometimes the duration of the pedal is marked with a horizontal line – the vertical line at the end shows where to release the pedal.

The next tune is shown using both methods so you can see them in context.

Long, Long Ago

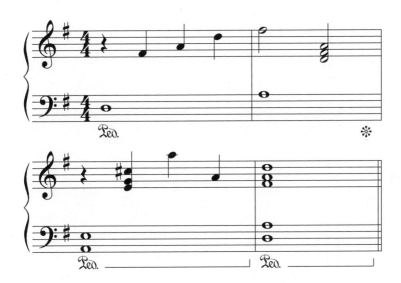

FREE ACCESS on smartphones, iPhone, Android etc.
Use any QR code app to scan this QR code

Or go straight to www.flametreemusic.com to
HEAR chords, scales, and find more resources

215

STEP
1

STEP
2

STEP
3

STEP
4

STEP
5

STEP
6

STEP
7

STEP
8

Right Hand Technique

There are many ways to improve your playing, both to make it sound better and to make it easier on the hands. This is where technique comes in.

Here are some reminders of the most important points:

1. Keep your **hand relaxed** (not tense).
2. **Fingers** should be **gently curved**.
3. Your **arm** should feel like it is **floating** along.

When you need to play fast, it is important to stay relaxed as if you let your hand get tense this will slow the muscles down.

1. For **fast runs** of notes, try to **keep your hand steady** and let your fingers do the work.
2. For **trills** (quick alternation between two notes) let your **hand rock a little**.
3. For lots of **staccato**, let your **wrist** help – don't try to just use the fingers.

The next tunes make use of fast runs and trills.

Allegro in D (Steinberger)

STEP 1

STEP 2

STEP 3

STEP 4

STEP 5

STEP 6

STEP 7

STEP 8

STEP 1

STEP 2

STEP 3

STEP 4

STEP 5

STEP 6

STEP 7

STEP 8

Gavotte (Gossec)

STEP
1

STEP
2

STEP
3

STEP
4

STEP
5

STEP
6

STEP
7

STEP
8

STEP
1

STEP
2

STEP
3

STEP
4

STEP
5

STEP
6

STEP
7

STEP
8

What We Know So Far

In the earlier sections we learned about pitches and lengths, and we also learned about different ways of moving around the keyboard. This section has introduced the following:

1. **Dynamics** – music can be loud, soft or somewhere in between.

2. Letters, which stand for **Italian words**, **indicate** how **loud** or **soft** to **play**.

3. Notes can be smooth (**legato**) or detached (**staccato**).

4. **Legato** music can be indicated by a curved line called a slur.

5. **Staccato** notes are indicated with a dot above or below them.

6. The **left pedal** helps you play **quietly**.

7. The **right pedal sustains** the notes played.

8. **Good technique** will help you play better.

FREE ACCESS on smartphones, iPhone, Android etc. Use any QR code app to scan this QR code

Or go straight to www.flametreemusic.com to **HEAR** chords, scales, and find more resources

Now Try This

Let's put all these new ideas together. The music that follows has all the indications you would expect in a complete piece of music. These indications help you to play the music exactly as the composer intended.

Try playing some of these tunes completely ignoring all the dynamics and other markings. Then play them with everything included. Can you hear how much better the music sounds when you follow all the dynamics and other markings?

We will add just one more symbol – a shorthand way of writing quickly alternating notes. It is called a **trill**.

Notice that you need to fit in an extra note near the end (called the **turn**) in order for the trill to flow **smoothly** into the next note. The number of notes you can fit in will depend on the style and speed of the music.

This is what the **trill sign** looks like...

...and this is how you play it

STEP 1

STEP 2

STEP 3

STEP 4

STEP 5

STEP 6

STEP 7

STEP 8

The Merry Peasant

FREE ACCESS on smartphones, iPhone, Android etc. Use any QR code app to scan this QR code Or go straight to www.flametreemusic.com to **HEAR** chords, scales, and find more resources

STEP 1

STEP 2

STEP 3

STEP 4

STEP 5

STEP 6

STEP 7

STEP 8

German Dance (Weber)

STEP
1

STEP
2

STEP
3

STEP
4

STEP
5

STEP
6

STEP
7

STEP
8

STEP 1

STEP 2

STEP 3

STEP 4

STEP 5

STEP 6

STEP 7

STEP 8

Mazurka in B Flat (Chopin)

FREE ACCESS on smartphones, iPhone, Android etc.
Use any QR code app to scan this QR code

Or go straight to www.flametreemusic.com to
HEAR chords, scales, and find more resources

224

STEP 1

STEP 2

STEP 3

STEP 4

STEP 5

STEP 6

STEP 7

STEP 8

Rondo in D (Mozart)

Notice the clef for the left hand in this piece

Or go straight to www.flametreemusic.com to **HEAR** chords, scales, and find more resources

STEP 1

STEP 2

STEP 3

STEP 4

STEP 5

STEP 6

STEP 7

STEP 8

STEP 8

FURTHER TECHNIQUES

This section will expand on the knowledge you have already, and in turn this will open up much more music to you. We will add a few more key signatures, scales and chords to your repertoire covering up to five sharps and five flats. We have covered scales, but these were mainly the major scales. This section looks at minor and chromatic scales. Arpeggios will also be expanded.

Finally, we have some more practice at playing by ear and further left-hand techniques.

STEP 1

STEP 2

STEP 3

STEP 4

STEP 5

STEP 6

STEP 7

STEP 8

FREE ACCESS on smartphones, iPhone, Android etc. Use any QR code app to scan this QR code

Or go straight to www.flametreemusic.com to **HEAR** chords, scales, and find more resources

229

More Key Signatures

So far we have used up to two sharps or two flats in key signatures. We will now add key signatures with up to five sharps or flats.

As mentioned when key signatures were first introduced, they can indicate either a major or minor key. The minor key (known as the '**relative minor**') for a particular key signature can be found by **counting down three half steps (semitones)** from the **major key**. A 'half step' is the distance from one note to the very next one, irrespective of whether it is black or white. So the relative minor of C major is A minor.

The chart below shows all the key signatures up to five sharps or flats and indicates both the major and minor names. We will follow this with two tunes, each using one of the new key signatures.

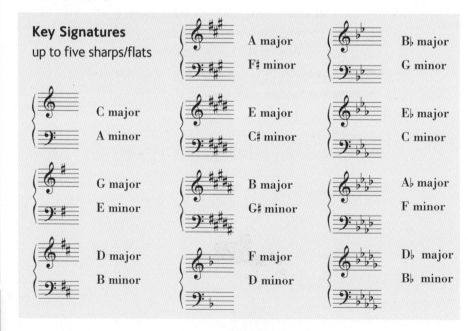

Key Signatures
up to five sharps/flats

A major / F♯ minor — B♭ major / G minor

C major / A minor — E major / C♯ minor — E♭ major / C minor

G major / E minor — B major / G♯ minor — A♭ major / F minor

D major / B minor — F major / D minor — D♭ major / B♭ minor

Finale from Sonata in A (Haydn)

STEP
1

STEP
2

STEP
3

STEP
4

STEP
5

STEP
6

STEP
7

STEP
8

Harmonic Minor Scales

Major scales are pretty straightforward to play – you just play all the notes from the root note, over one octave, making notes sharp or flat according to the key signature.

Minor scales are slightly different in that you need to make a small adjustment to the notes. Don't worry – it is the same change for all keys.

In the **harmonic minor scale**, you start on the root note – but when you get to the **seventh note** you need to **sharpen it**. If the note starts off as a white note then that is easy, but if it is a flat then you need to remember that it will become a natural (to sharpen a note you move it one to the right).

Look at the examples opposite and you will see.

There are just a few additional time signatures and symbols to learn, which will increase the range of music you can play.

| 3 quavers per bar | 9 quavers per bar | 12 quavers per bar | 2 minims per bar |

FREE ACCESS on smartphones, iPhone, Android etc. Use any QR code app to scan this QR code

Or go straight to www.flametreemusic.com to **HEAR** chords, scales, and find more resources

A harmonic minor

sharpened 7th

D harmonic minor

sharpened 7th

B flat harmonic minor

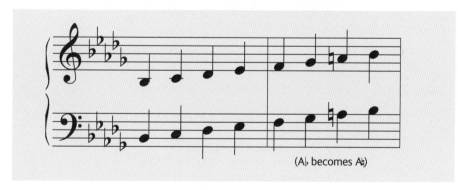

(A♭ becomes A♮)

Or go straight to www.flametreemusic.com to
HEAR chords, scales, and find more resources

STEP
1

STEP
2

STEP
3

STEP
4

STEP
5

STEP
6

STEP
7

STEP
8

Chromatic Scales

The final type of scale we will introduce is the chromatic scale.

The chromatic scale is basically **every note** within an **octave**, black and white.

Here is a chromatic scale:

Chromatic Scale on C

Opposite are a few exercises to practise chromatic passages.

Also, play the tunes on the following pages, which use sections of minor scales and chromatic scales – see if you can spot them.

FREE ACCESS on smartphones, iPhone, Android etc. Use any QR code app to scan this QR code

Or go straight to www.flametreemusic.com to **HEAR** chords, scales, and find more resources

STEP 1
STEP 2
STEP 3
STEP 4
STEP 5
STEP 6
STEP 7
STEP 8

Chromatic Exercise 1

Chromatic Exercise 2

Mazurka in G Minor (Chopin)

FREE ACCESS on smartphones, iPhone, Android etc.
Use any QR code app to scan this QR code

Or go straight to www.flametreemusic.com to
HEAR chords, scales, and find more resources

Sarabande (Bach)

STEP 1

STEP 2

STEP 3

STEP 4

STEP 5

STEP 6

STEP 7

STEP 8

FREE ACCESS on smartphones, iPhone, Android etc. Use any QR code app to scan this QR code

Or go straight to www.flametreemusic.com to **HEAR** chords, scales, and find more resources

STEP
1

STEP
2

STEP
3

STEP
4

STEP
5

STEP
6

STEP
7

STEP
8

More Arpeggios

Here are arpeggios in some of the new keys we now know.

Look carefully at the fingering, as this will help you move around the keyboard smoothly and without having to jump.

Most arpeggios will fit into one of these fingering patterns.

We will follow this with an arpeggio-style exercise so you can practise this technique, then a tune to help you play by ear – listen to the music, then fill in the gaps with suitable arpeggios.

C D

E major arpeggio

E flat major arpeggio

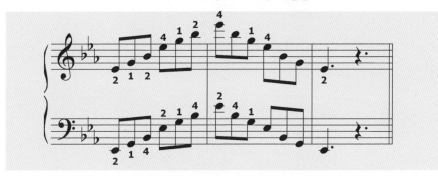

B flat minor arpeggio

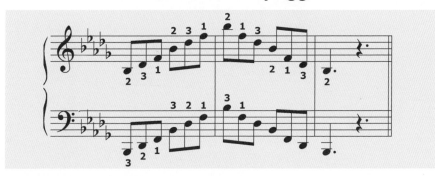

Or go straight to www.flametreemusic.com to **HEAR** chords, scales, and find more resources

STEP 1

STEP 2

STEP 3

STEP 4

STEP 5

STEP 6

STEP 7

STEP 8

Arpeggio Exercise

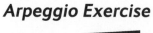

Fill The Gaps

STEP 1
STEP 2
STEP 3
STEP 4
STEP 5
STEP 6
STEP 7
STEP 8

STEP
1

STEP
2

STEP
3

STEP
4

STEP
5

STEP
6

STEP
7

STEP
8

Improvizing

As well as being able to play exactly what the composer has written down on the page, it is a useful skill to be able to improvize.

Improvizing need not be a frightening subject – you can make it as complicated or simple as you want. The most important thing to remember is to listen.

Listen carefully and think about what you want to play – improvizing is in reality always planned. You might only plan what you are going to play a fraction of a second before you play it, but you should always know what sound your fingers will make before you press the keys.

The next few pages give you tips and guidance on improvizing techniques.

You will have something to start from – something to 'improvize over'. This is usually a **chord chart**. Here is a check list of what to look for:

- ✪ Look at the chords and make sure you know the notes for all of them.

- ✪ Think about the style and speed of the music – do the chords change very quickly or will you be on each chord for a few beats?

- ✪ Look for common notes in consecutive chords – this will help you join them together better.

- ✪ Can you see a bass line going through the chords?

- ✪ What sort of accompaniment are you going to play?

FREE ACCESS on smartphones, iPhone, Android etc. Use any QR code app to scan this QR code

Or go straight to www.flametreemusic.com to **HEAR** chords, scales, and find more resources

Let's take a look at a simple chord progression:

First play the root chords in both hands.

Now let's try playing them in inversion so we don't have to jump around.

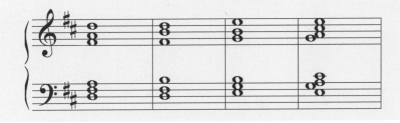

If we want a 'walking bass' then we need to see if there is a smooth route between the chords.

STEP 1
STEP 2
STEP 3
STEP 4
STEP 5
STEP 6
STEP 7
STEP 8

STEP
1

STEP
2

STEP
3

STEP
4

STEP
5

STEP
6

STEP
7

STEP
8

Now let's try a similar thing in the right hand, but we can add notes of different lengths to make it more interesting.

Next, let's see if we can combine the two. Play the tune and the bass line and include a few harmony notes.

The next page has some chord charts for you to practise with. Keep the check list in mind and work your way through them. Start simple, then make them more adventurous when you have got the hang of it.

FREE ACCESS on smartphones, iPhone, Android etc. Use any QR code app to scan this QR code

Or go straight to www.flametreemusic.com to **HEAR** chords, scales, and find more resources

$\frac{4}{4}$ E | E7 | A | F#m

F# | B | B7 | E

$\frac{3}{4}$ F | Dm | B♭ | C7

F | B♭ | C7 | F

$\frac{4}{4}$ C | Em | F | C

F | D7 | G7 | C

STEP 1

STEP 2

STEP 3

STEP 4

STEP 5

STEP 6

STEP 7

STEP 8

FREE ACCESS on smartphones, iPhone, Android etc. Use any QR code app to scan this QR code

Or go straight to www.flametreemusic.com to **HEAR** chords, scales, and find more resources

STEP
1

STEP
2

STEP
3

STEP
4

STEP
5

STEP
6

STEP
7

STEP
8

Left-hand Techniques

More often than not, you will have a melody in the right hand and need to accompany that melody in the left hand.

Here are a few options; look back at the music you have already played and see if you can spot each technique.

1. **Single notes.**

2. **Simple chords.**

3. **Broken chords and arpeggios.**

4. **Melodic lines that 'fit in' with the tune.**

Opposite are some examples of left-hand accompaniment styles. The tunes on the following pages use one of these techniques.

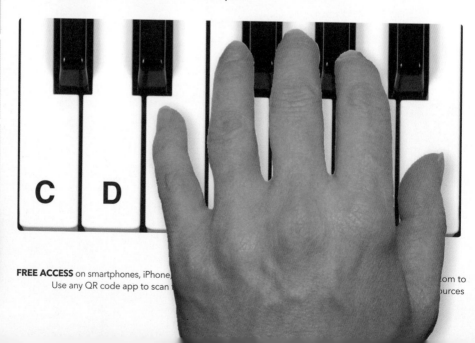

C   D

FREE ACCESS on smartphones, iPhone, ~~~~~~~~~~~~~~~~~~~~~~~~~~~~~~~~~~~~~om to
Use any QR code app to scan ~~~~~~~~~~~~~~~~~~~~~~~~~~~~~~~~~~~~~ources

Simple chordal accompaniment

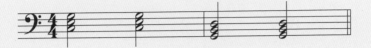

Bass note plus chord

Broken chord (keeps in hand position)

Arpeggio (uses a wider range on the keyboard)

Broken chord (wider range and with rhythmic pattern)

Bass note and chord (with rhythmic pattern)

STEP 1

STEP 2

STEP 3

STEP 4

STEP 5

STEP 6

STEP 7

STEP 8

FREE ACCESS on smartphones, iPhone, Android etc. Use any QR code app to scan this QR code

Or go straight to www.flametreemusic.com to **HEAR** chords, scales, and find more resources

STEP
1

STEP
2

STEP
3

STEP
4

STEP
5

STEP
6

STEP
7

STEP
8

Scherzo (Schubert)

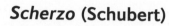

FREE ACCESS on smartphones, iPhone, Android etc.
Use any QR code app to scan this QR code

Or go straight to www.flametreemusic.com to
HEAR chords, scales, and find more resources

248

Berceuse (Chopin)

FREE ACCESS on smartphones, iPhone, Android etc.
Use any QR code app to scan this QR code

Or go straight to www.flametreemusic.com to
HEAR chords, scales, and find more resources

249

STEP 1
STEP 2
STEP 3
STEP 4
STEP 5
STEP 6
STEP 7
STEP 8

STEP
1

STEP
2

STEP
3

STEP
4

STEP
5

STEP
6

STEP
7

STEP
8

What We Know So Far

This section has significantly increased your musical knowledge. We have covered key signatures up to five sharps and flats, looked at left-hand technique, learned about different styles of music and introduced improvization.

That is a lot of information to take in. Read through the following points to remind you about all this.

1. Key signatures have either **sharps** or **flats**.

2. Each key signature represents one **major** and one **minor** key.

3. The **relative minor** is 3 **half-steps** (semitones) **below** the **major**.

4. **Harmonic minor scales** have a **sharpened 7th.**

5. **Chromatic** scales use **all** the black and white **notes.**

6. **Fingering** is important when playing **arpeggios**.

7. It is important to **listen** carefully when **improvizing**.

8. There are a small number of common **left-hand techniques** which can be used when **accompanying a melody.**

FREE ACCESS on smartphones, iPhone, Android etc.
Use any QR code app to scan this QR code

Or go straight to www.flametreemusic.com to
HEAR chords, scales, and find more resources

Now Try This

If you go to the Flame Tree Red Book in the Pieces section (online at flametreemusic.com), you will be able to consolidate what you have learned in this section.

There are tunes in the new keys, and some will be in the minor – **look out for accidentals** which may indicate the **sharpened 7th.**

Also look at the **left-hand parts**: see if you can spot the accompaniment techniques you have learned. **Look for chords** and also for **chord shapes** made up from consecutive notes. Are these broken chords?

When you **see** a **row** of **notes**, try to **work out** *which* **scale** they are from. They could be major, minor or chromatic. They will most often come from the scale associated with the key signature of the music.

As always, **practise each hand separately** before trying to put them together.

Repeat Sign

The music between these two signs should be repeated. If the first symbol above is not present then you should repeat from the beginning.

Accent

This sign means you should play the note a little louder.

STEP 1

STEP 2

STEP 3

STEP 4

STEP 5

STEP 6

STEP 7

STEP 8

FREE ACCESS on smartphones, iPhone, Android etc. Use any QR code app to scan this QR code

Or go straight to www.flametreemusic.com to **HEAR** chords, scales, and find more resources

THE NEXT STEP

GOING ONLINE

And finally you can go to www.flametreemusic.com where you can find and listen to chords, scales and other resources to help you learn more as a musician and piano player.

FREE ACCESS on smartphones, iPhone, Android etc.
Use any QR code app to scan this QR code

Or go straight to www.flametreemusic.com to **HEAR** chords, scales, and find more resources

253

STEP
1

STEP
2

STEP
3

STEP
4

STEP
5

STEP
6

STEP
7

STEP
8

FlameTreeMusic.com gives you a number of resources to complement this book:

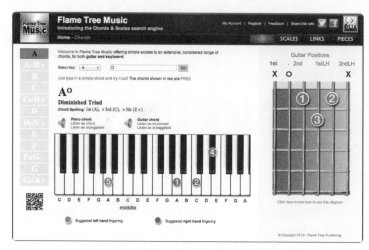

- A wide range of chords which can be **heard** in piano and guitar sounds.
- 20 core scales are provided for each key, again you can **hear** the notes played on the guitar and the piano.

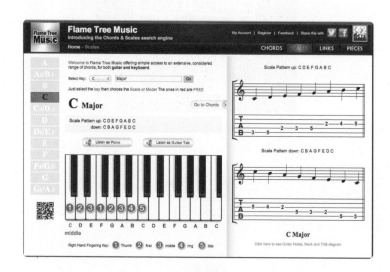

FREE ACCESS on smartphones, iPhone, Android etc. Use any QR code app to scan this QR code

Or go straight to www.flametreemusic.com to **HEAR** chords, scales, and find more resources